Department of Health
Department for Education and Employment
Home Office

Framework for the Assessment of Children in Need and their Families

London

The Stationery Office

Social Care Group

The Social Care Group is one of four business groups in the Department of Health. It is jointly headed by the Chief Social Services Inspector and the Head of Social Care Policy. It supports Ministers in promoting high quality, cost effective services through

- national policies

- support to external social care agencies

- inspection

The Social Services Inspectorate is a part of the Social Care Group. It is headed by the Chief Social Services Inspector who is the principal professional advisor to Ministers on social services and related matters.

Web Access

This document is available on the DoH internet web site at:
http://www.open.gov.uk/doh/quality.htm

This publication is also available on The Stationery Office website at
https://www.the-stationery-office.co.uk/doh/ facn/facn.htm

The Stationery Office site contains the document in a fully searchable format together with links to related publications referenced in the text. The data is held on a secure site that is password protected so you will need the following infomation to access it:
User name: facneed
Password: r4ch7rd
Please note that both fields are case sensitive and contain no spaces.

© Crown copyright 2000

First published 2000

Published with permission of Department of Health on behalf of the Controller of Her Majesty's Stationery Office.

ISBN 0 11 322310 2

Published by The Stationery Office Ltd

Applications for reproduction should be made in writing to:
The Copyright Unit
Her Majesty's Stationery Office
St Clements House
2–16 Colegate
Norwich NR3 1BQ

Printed in the United Kingdom for The Stationery Office
TJ000912 c1050 04/00 (6157)

Contents

Appendices

Foreword

We cannot begin to improve the lives of disadvantaged and vulnerable children unless we identify their needs and understand what is happening to them in order to take appropriate action.

The Government is committed to delivering better life chances to such children through a range of cross-cutting, inter-departmental initiatives. A key component of the Government's objectives for children's social services is the development of a framework for assessing children in need and their families, to ensure a timely response and the effective provision of services. This is being taken forward as part of the Quality Protects Programme.

Delivering services to children in need in our communities is a corporate responsibility. It falls on all local authority departments, health authorities and community services. Improvements in outcomes for children in need can only be achieved by close collaboration between professionals and agencies working with children and families. This Guidance reflects such collaboration and is issued jointly by the Department of Health, the Department for Education and Employment and the Home Office. It is issued under section 7 of the Local Authority Social Services Act 1970.

The Guidance draws widely on a wealth of research about the needs of children and the best of practice. Many people have contributed generously to its development and it has been substantially enriched by an extensive consultation exercise. It is intended to provide a valuable foundation for policy and practice for all those who manage and provide services to children in need and their families. This document is the cornerstone in a series of accompanying publications, materials and training resources about the assessment of children in need. The Assessment Framework has been incorporated into *Working Together to Safeguard Children*.

The value of this framework for assessing children in need and their families will be measured in future improvements in our responses to some of our most vulnerable children - children in need.

John Hutton
Minister of State for Social Services
March 2000

Preface

Securing the wellbeing of children by protecting them from all forms of harm and ensuring their developmental needs are responded to appropriately are primary aims of Government policy. Local authority social services departments working with other local authority departments and health authorities have a **duty to safeguard and promote the welfare of children in their area who are in need** and to promote the upbringing of such children, wherever possible by their families, through providing an appropriate range of services. A critical task is to ascertain with the family whether a child is in need and how that child and family might best be helped. The effectiveness with which a child's needs are assessed will be key to the effectiveness of subsequent actions and services and, ultimately, to the outcomes for the child.

A Framework for Assessing Children in Need

A framework has been developed which provides a systematic way of analysing, understanding and recording what is happening to children and young people within their families and the wider context of the community in which they live. From such an understanding of what are inevitably complex issues and inter-relationships, clear professional judgements can be made. These judgements include whether the child being assessed is in need, whether the child is suffering or likely to suffer significant harm, what actions must be taken and which services would best meet the needs of this particular child and family. The evidence based knowledge which has informed the development of the framework has been drawn from a wide range of research studies and theories across a number of disciplines and from the accumulated experience of policy and practice.

The Guidance describes the Assessment Framework and the Government's expectations of how it will be used. It reflects the principles contained within the United Nations Convention on the Rights of the Child, ratified by the UK Government in 1991 and the Human Rights Act 1998. In addition, it takes account of relevant legislation at the time of publication, but is particularly informed by the requirements of the Children Act 1989, which provides a comprehensive framework for the care and protection of children.

This document is issued under section 7 of the Local Authority Social Services Act 1970, which requires local authorities in their social services functions to act under the general guidance of the Secretary of State. As such this document does not have the full force of statute, but should be complied with unless local circumstances indicate exceptional reasons which justify a variation.

The Guidance is a key element of the Department of Health's work to support local authorities in implementing Quality Protects, the Government's programme for transforming the management and delivery of children's social services. Quality Protects aims to deliver better life chances for the most vulnerable and disadvantaged children, and good assessment lies at the heart of this work. The Government's consolidated set of objectives for children's social services published in September 1999 makes clear the importance of assessment in the work of local authority departments and health authorities. The framework has been incorporated into the Government Guidance on protecting children from harm, *Working Together to Safeguard Children* (Department of Health *et al*, 1999) and should be read in conjunction with it when there are concerns that a child may be or is suffering significant harm.

The Guidance is not a practice manual. It does not set out step-by-step procedures to be followed: rather it sets out a framework which should be adapted and used to suit individual circumstances. A range of additional publications has been produced to inform practitioners and their managers about the most up-to-date knowledge from research and practice. Practice guidance (Department of Health, 2000a) and a training pack consisting of a training video, guide and reader (NSPCC and University of Sheffield, 2000) have also been developed to accompany the Guidance and to assist the introduction and implementation of the new framework. The Department of Health will be working closely with local authorities, health services and other agencies through the Quality Protects Programme to help them put the framework into practice in the most cost effective way.

Who is the Guidance for?

The Guidance has been produced primarily for the use of professionals and other staff who will be involved in undertaking assessments of children in need and their families under the Children Act 1989. Social services departments have lead responsibility for assessments of children in need including those children who may be or are suffering significant harm but, under section 27 of the Children Act 1989, other local authority services and health authorities have a duty to assist social services in carrying out this function. These other agencies should be aware of the Assessment Framework and understand what it might mean for them.

Many agencies have contact with and responsibility for children and young people under a range of legislation. The Guidance is, therefore, also relevant to assessments concerned with the welfare of children in a number of contexts.

Health, education and youth justice services, in particular, may have already had considerable involvement with some children and families prior to referral to social services departments. They will have an important contribution to make to the assessment and, where appropriate, to the provision of services to those families. Their awareness of the Assessment Framework when contributing to assessments of children in need will facilitate communication between agencies and with children and families. It will also assist the process of referral from one agency to another and increase the likelihood of acceptance of the contents of previous assessments, thereby reducing unnecessary duplication of assessment and increasing local confidence in inter-agency work. Knowledge of the Assessment Framework can inform contributions by all agencies and disciplines when assessing children about whom there are child safety concerns (Paragraphs 5.13 and 5.33 in *Working Together to Safeguard Children*, 1999).

Effective collaborative work between staff of different disciplines and agencies assessing children in need and their families requires a common language to understand the needs of children, shared values about what is in children's best interests and a joint commitment to improving the outcomes for children. The framework for assessment provides that common language based on explicit values about children, knowledge about what children need to ensure their successful development, and the factors in their lives which may positively or negatively influence their upbringing. This increases the likelihood of parents and children experiencing consistency between professionals and themselves about what will be important for children's wellbeing and healthy development.

Government Guidance on promoting independence in adult social services, *Achieving Fairer Access to Adult Social Care Services* (Department of Health, forthcoming, a) will address how to respond to social services referrals regarding adults. With any adult referral, social services should check whether the person has parenting responsibilities for a child under 18. If so, the initial assessment should explore any parenting and child related issues in accordance with the *Framework for the Assessment of Children in Need and their Families* Guidance and provide services as appropriate. The needs of the adult should be assessed in accordance with *Achieving Fair Access to Adult Social Care Services*.

The Policy Context

The Government is committed to ending child poverty, tackling social exclusion and promoting the welfare of all children – so that they can thrive and have the opportunity to fulfil their potential as citizens throughout their lives. There are a number of programmes such as Sure Start, Connexions and Quality Protects and a range of policies to support families, promote educational attainment, reduce truancy and school exclusion and secure a future for all young people in education, employment or training. They all aim to ensure that children and families most at risk of social exclusion have every opportunity to build successful, independent lives.

At the same time, the Government is committed to improving the quality and management of those services responsible for supporting children and families particularly through the modernisation of social services, through the promotion of co-operation between all statutory agencies and through building effective partnerships with voluntary and private agencies.

Promoting the wellbeing of children to ensure optimal outcomes requires integration at both national and local levels: joined up government – in respect both of policy making and of service delivery – is central to the current extensive policy agenda. A Ministerial Group on the Family, supported by the Family Policy Unit in the Home Office, encourages this approach at Government level. Its aim is to provide a new emphasis on looking more widely at the needs of all children and families in the community and to develop a programme of measures which will strengthen family life.

Early intervention is essential to support children and families before problems, either from within the family or as a result of external factors, which have an impact on parenting capacity and family life escalate into crisis or abuse. Government departments, statutory and voluntary agencies, academics and practitioners contribute to this work. Good joint working practices and understanding at a local level are vital to the success of the early intervention agenda. Local agencies, including schools and education support services, social services departments, youth offending teams, primary and more specialist health care services and voluntary and private agencies should work together to establish agreed referral protocols which will help to ensure that early indications of a child being at risk of social exclusion receive appropriate attention.

The development of a framework for assessing children in need and their families will contribute to integrated working. The new framework was announced by the Secretary of State for Health in September 1998. Its primary purpose is to improve outcomes for children in need. It is also designed to assist local authority departments and health authorities meet one of the Government's objectives for children's social services (Department of Health, 1999e) - to ensure that referral and assessment processes discriminate effectively between different types and levels of need, and produce a timely service response.

The Contents of the Guidance

The Guidance starts by outlining the legislation, responsibilities and principles which underpin the work of local authority departments and health authorities in promoting and safeguarding children's welfare and assessing children's needs. It then describes the framework and the assessment process in more detail in Chapters 2, 3 and 4. There is reference to the needs of children in general and to children who may have specific needs and impairments throughout the Guidance. Roles and responsibilities in inter-agency assessment are described in Chapter 5. The Guidance concludes by considering the organisational arrangements which should be in place to support effective assessment of children in need.

Relationship to Previous Guidance on Assessment

This Guidance builds on and supersedes earlier Department of Health guidance on assessing children, *Protecting Children: A Guide for Social Workers undertaking a Comprehensive Assessment* (1988). That publication (often referred to as the 'Orange Book') has been widely used by social work practitioners as a guide to comprehensive assessment for long term planning in child protection cases. Its purpose was to assist social work practitioners, in consultation with other agencies, to understand the child and family's situation more fully once concerns about significant harm had been established following initial enquiries and assessment. Much of its thinking about children's development and parents' capacity to respond to children's needs has been incorporated into the Assessment Framework.

However, over the years concerns have arisen about the use made of *Protecting Children*. Inspections and research have shown that the guide was sometimes followed mechanistically and used as a check list, without any differentiation according to the child's or family's circumstances. Assessment was regarded as an event rather than as a process and services were withheld awaiting the completion of an assessment. In some authorities, an all or nothing approach was found; either very detailed comprehensive assessments were carried out or there was no record of any analysis of the child and the family's circumstances. The framework for assessing children in need and their families contained in this volume is underpinned by a set of principles which seek to remedy any misunderstandings about the task of working with children and families in order to understand what is happening to them and how they might best be helped.

Effective Implementation

A range of organisational arrangements need to be in place to ensure sound practice in using the framework for assessing children in need and their families. The effectiveness of assessment processes will be measurable over time by evidence of improving outcomes for children and families known to social services departments. The Department of Health will be working closely with all those involved in providing services to children to develop appropriate arrangements at national and local level, to learn from the experiences of children and families and to evaluate the impact this approach to assessment is having on outcomes for children in need.

1

Children in Need

Children and Families in England

1.1   There are approximately eleven million children in England. It is estimated that over four million of them are living in families with less than half the average household income. By other calculations, well over three million children are living in poverty (Utting, 1995). Where these children live is significant. 'Over the last generation, this has become a divided country. While most areas have benefited from rising living standards, the poorest neighbourhoods have tended to become more run down, more prone to crime and more cut off from the labour market' (Social Exclusion Unit, 1998). Estimates vary about how many neighbourhoods are in the poorest categories, ranging from 1,600 to 4,000 in Britain as a whole. In response to these trends, the Government is developing major strategies to tackle the root causes of poverty and social exclusion, and to respond to the serious and multi-faceted problems for children and their families which these can create, particularly in the poorest areas. These strategies also aim to encourage and promote preventive and early intervention approaches to help reduce the scale and difficulty of such problems and to tackle them before they become entrenched.

1.2   Just as the problems facing families are often interlinked, so the services provided for children and their families need to work closely together to be most effective. Everyone benefits if services are properly co-ordinated and integrated. It is the purpose of Children's Services Planning (Department of Health and Department for Education and Employment,1996) to identify the broad range and level of need in an area and to develop corporate, inter-agency, community based plans of action to provide the most effective network of services within the resources available. It is important that all those concerned with services to children and families – statutory and voluntary bodies, community groups and families – contribute to the development of these plans.

1.3   It is recognised that many families are under considerable stress, that being a parent is hard work, and families have a right to expect practical support from universal services, such as health and education. The importance of all parents having available to them good quality local resources is acknowledged. The Government is committed to supporting parenting and has set up the National Family and Parenting Institute to assess the support needs of families, to raise public awareness of the importance of parenting and the needs of children, to map and disseminate information and good practice, and to provide advice to Government and others in a way which reflects our culturally diverse society. It will work collaboratively with others to help develop parent support services and to influence the research agenda and analyse and disseminate research findings. It will draw on anonymised data from ParentLine Plus, whose freephone national telephone Helpline is available to provide a service to all parents. Steps are being taken through public service and welfare reforms to modernise the National Health Service, raise standards in local schools, provide good out of school care, reduce crime, ensure streets are safe for families and strengthen communities' capacities to respond to and support families. This forms an ambitious programme which will take many years to deliver in full and requires continuous concerted central and local government effort.

1.4   All families may experience difficulties from time to time for a whole host of reasons which may have an impact on their children. These reasons may include the death of a family member, physical or mental ill health in the family, the breakdown of marital or other significant relationships, sudden loss of employment, multiple births, or having a child with special educational needs. Not all adults are well prepared for the daily upheavals and stress of bringing up a child. Some parents may find one particular stage in their child's life especially stressful, for example adolescence. Many cope well enough with one problem but a combination of problems can have a cummulative debilitating effect.

1.5   Many families coping with extremely difficult circumstances receive sufficient support from friends, relatives and services in the community including universal services to overcome potential disadvantage. They are not likely to seek or require additional services. In this sense, parenting has been called 'a buffered system' (Belsky and Vondra, 1989). In some cases the buffers of family and community resources may not exist or be sufficient to ensure the current or future wellbeing of the child. It is in these situations that additional support or services may be necessary, some of which may be purchased by parents (such as day care) or obtained directly from other statutory or voluntary agencies (such as befriending by a volunteer). Some parents may turn to or be referred to child welfare agencies in the community and require targeted services from health, education and social services.

The Extent of Children in Need

1.6   Children may be defined as in need in many different circumstances. The information on how many children are known to social services is not available nationally, but current estimates suggest between 300,000 and 400,000 children are known at any one time. Figure 1 shows how the extent of need can be represented within the context of vulnerable[1] and all children. According to Department of Health statistics, about 53,000 children are looked after in statutory care at any one time (Department of Health, 1999b). This figure excludes those disabled children receiving respite care. Approximately 32,000 children's names are on a Child Protection Register at any one time because they require a child protection plan (Department of Health, 1999i).

1.7   The families referred to or seeking help from social services will have differing levels of need. Many will be helped by advice or practical services or short term intervention. A smaller proportion will have problems of such complexity and seriousness that they

---

1. Vulnerable children are those disadvantaged children who would benefit from extra help from public agencies in order to make the best of their life chances. Four million children live in families with less than half the average household income.

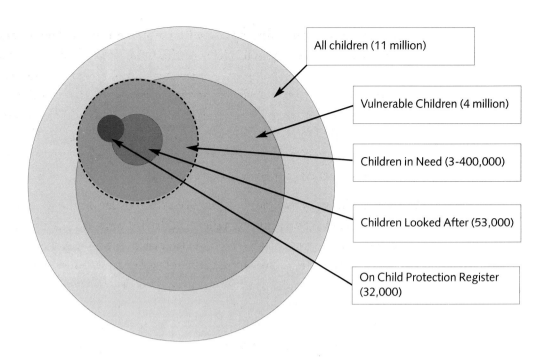

All children (11 million)

Vulnerable Children (4 million)

Children in Need (3-400,000)

Children Looked After (53,000)

On Child Protection Register (32,000)

Figure 1 **Representation of Extent of Children in Need in England at any one time**

require more detailed assessment, involving other agencies in that process, leading to appropriate plans and interventions.

1.8   This can best be illustrated by examining the experience of one unitary authority, as an example:

EXAMPLE: UNITARY AUTHORITY 1997–1999	1997/98	1998/99
Total child population under the age of 18	35,086	35,086
Children referred to social services as children in need	4.000	4,097
Child Protection s47 enquiries carried out	1,752	708
Total number of children on Child Protection Register at year end	161	96
Total number of children looked after at year end	217	202

1.9   This authority, in parallel with many others, has been working for the past three years with its community and local agencies to take a broader-based approach to helping vulnerable children and their families and has begun to find:

- a slight increase in child care referrals;

- the majority of referrals more appropriately dealt with under s17;

- proportionally fewer child protection s47 enquiries;

- fewer children's names being placed on the child protection register;

- a decrease in the numbers of children being looked after;

- a decrease in the numbers of children accommodated on an unplanned basis;

- a reduction in the anxiety levels of all staff in child and family work.

1.10 Ensuring that assessment discriminates effectively between different types and levels of need, from the point of referral onwards, is critical to the objective of improving the effectiveness of services to children and securing best value from available resources (Department of Health, 1999e).

Children in Need under the Children Act 1989

1.11 The obligations of the State to assist families who need help in bringing up their own children are laid down in legislation. Part III of the Children Act 1989 is the basis in law for the provision of local services to children in need: children in this respect are defined as under the age of 18 (s105).

> *It shall be the general duty of every local authority –*
> - *to safeguard and promote the welfare of children within their area who are in need; and*
> - *so far as is consistent with that duty, to promote the upbringing of such children by their families, by providing a range and level of services appropriate to those children's needs.*
>
> **Children Act 1989 s17(1)**

1.12 The Children Act 1989 places a specific duty on agencies to co-operate in the interests of children in need in section 27. Section 322 of the Education Act 1996 also places a duty on the local authority to assist the local education authority where any child who has special educational needs.

> *Where it appears to a local authority that any authority or other person mentioned in sub-section (3) could, by taking any specified action, help in the exercise of any of their functions under this Part, they may request the help of that other authority or persons, specifying the action in question.*
>
> *An authority whose help is so requested shall comply with the request if it is compatible with their own statutory or other duties and obligations and does not unduly prejudice the discharge of any of their functions.*
>
> *The persons are –*
> a. *any local authority;*
> b. *any local education authority;*
> c. *any local housing authority;*
> d. *any health authority, special health authority, National Health Services Trust or Primary Care Trust; and*
> e. *any person authorised by the Secretary of State for the purpose of this section.*
>
> **Children Act 1989 s27**

1.13 Several key principles which underpin the Children Act 1989 are found in Part III of the Act:

- it is the duty of the State through local authorities to **both safeguard and promote the welfare of vulnerable children**;

- it is in the children's best interests to be brought up in their own families wherever possible;

- whilst it is parents' responsibility to bring up their children, they may need assistance from time to time to do so;

- they should be able to call upon services, including accommodation (under s20 of the Children Act 1989), from or with the help of the local authority when they are required.

The notion of partnership between State and families is thus also established in this Part of the Act.

1.14 In order to carry out these duties the meaning of **safeguarding** and **promoting** within the parameters of the Children Act 1989 should be appreciated, as should the contribution of these objectives to strengthening and supplementing parental capacities so that children may grow up in their families, wherever possible.

1.15 Safeguarding has two elements:

- a duty to protect children from maltreatment;

- a duty to prevent impairment.

1.16 The duty to protect children from maltreatment demands knowledge and understanding of the law and the accompanying government guidance, *Working Together to Safeguard Children* (1999).

1.17 However, safeguarding children should not be seen as a separate activity from promoting their welfare. They are two sides of the same coin. Promoting welfare has a wider, more positive, action centred approach embedded in a philosophy of creating opportunities to enable children to have optimum life chances in adulthood, as well as ensuring they are growing up in circumstances consistent with the provision of safe and effective care. A useful framework for looking at the policy context of children in need and the value of applying a twin approach of safeguarding and promoting welfare at different levels of intervention has been developed by Hardiker *et al* (1996; 1999). Their grid, reproduced in Appendix B, can be used to help the planning and appropriate provision of services.

1.18 Children who are defined as in need under the Children Act 1989 are those whose vulnerability is such that they are unlikely to reach or maintain a satisfactory level of health and development, or their health and development will be significantly impaired without the provision of services. The critical factors to be taken into account in deciding whether a child is in need under the Children Act 1989 are what will happen to a child's health and development **without services**, and the likely effect the services will have on the child's standard of health and development. Determining who is in need, what those needs are, and how services will have an effect on outcomes for children requires professional judgement by social services staff together with colleagues from other professional disciplines who are working with children and families.

1.19 The criteria for defining who is in need are spelt out above in section 17(10) of the Children Act 1989. The criteria include a child who is disabled. A child is defined as disabled *'if he is blind, deaf or dumb or suffers from mental disorder of any kind, or is substantially and permanently handicapped by illness, injury or congenital or other such disability as may be prescribed'* (s17(11)). This definition does not preclude children whose impairment may be less substantial from being defined as children in need under the other categories. Thus, where the family, educational, social or environmental circumstances may be preventing such a disabled child from achieving or maintaining a reasonable standard of health or development without the provision of services, the local authority should consider whether that child is a child in need.

> *A child shall be taken to be in need if –*
>
> a. *he is unlikely to achieve or maintain or to have the opportunity of achieving or maintaining, a reasonable standard of health or development without the provision for him of services by a local authority …*
>
> b. *his health or development is likely to be significantly impaired, or further impaired, without the provision for him of such services; or*
>
> c. *he is disabled,*
>
> *And "family" in relation to such a child, includes any person who has parental responsibility for the child and any other person with whom he has been living.*
>
> **Children Act 1989 s17(10)**

Assessing Children in Need

1.20 The duties and powers of the local authority to assess the needs of a child and to provide services are outlined in Part III of the Children Act 1989, in particular section 17, and Schedule 2 Part I. Part III is the main part of the Act (titled *Local Authority Support for Children and Families*) about the delivery of services by social services departments. Other Parts (I, II, IV and V) outline the way in which court orders may be obtained to authorise or enforce certain actions, in relation to family proceedings, care and supervision and the protection of children.

1.21 The Act gives local authority social services the power to assess children's needs as follows:

> *Where it appears to a local authority that a child within their area is in need, the authority may assess his needs for the purposes of this Act at the same time as any assessment of his needs is made under:*
>
> ● *the Chronically Sick and Disabled Persons Act 1970;*
>
> ● *the Education Act 1996;*
>
> ● *the Disabled Persons (Services, Consultation and Representation) Act 1986; or*
>
> ● *any other enactment.*
>
> **Children Act 1989 (Schedule 2, paragraph 3)**

1.22 Professionals from a number of agencies, but in particular health and education, are a key source of referral to social services departments of children who are, or may be, in need. They may already know these children and their families well and, if so, they will be key in assisting social services departments to carry out their assessment functions under the Children Act 1989. Knowledge of the Assessment Framework will be of use to all professionals when they are contributing to assessments of children in need, including when they are undertaking or contributing to assessments as part of their responsibilities for safeguarding children under *Working Together to Safeguard Children* (1999).

1.23 The following principles should guide inter-agency, inter-disciplinary work with children in need. It is essential to be clear about:

- the purpose and anticipated outputs from the assessment;

- the legislative basis for the assessment;

- the protocols and procedures to be followed;

- which agency, team or professional has lead responsibility;

- how the child and family members will be involved in the assessment process;

- which professional has lead responsibility for analysing the assessment findings and constructing a plan;

- the respective roles of each professional involved in the assessment;

- the way in which information will be shared across professional boundaries and within agencies, and be recorded;

- which professional will have responsibility for taking forward the plan when it is agreed.

1.24 It is important to agree an assessment plan with the child and family, so that all parties understand who is doing what, when, and how the various assessments will be used to inform overall judgements about a child's needs and subsequent planning. When joint assessments are being undertaken, clarity is required about whether this means one professional will undertake an assessment on behalf of the team or whether several types of assessment are to be undertaken in parallel. In the latter situation, thought is required regarding how these can be organised to avoid duplication. Service users, in particular parents of disabled children, report that assessments are often repetitive and uninformed by previous work. The agreed process should be based on what is appropriate for the needs of the particular child and family, taking account of the purpose of the assessment, rather than what fits best with professional systems. Agreed protocols and procedures should be flexible enough to accommodate different ways of undertaking assessments within the overall Assessment Framework.

Children Who are Suffering or are Likely to Suffer Significant Harm

1.25 Some children are in need because they are suffering or likely to suffer significant harm. Concerns about maltreatment may be the reason for referral of a family to social services or concerns may arise during the course of providing services to a family. In such circumstances, the local authority is obliged to consider initiating enquiries to find out what is happening to a child and whether action should be taken to protect a child. This obligation is set out in Part V s47 of the Children Act 1989 *(Protection of Children)*:

1.26 This section of the Act requires local authorities to consider if action is necessary. To make enquiries implies the need to assess what is happening to a child. The procedures for such action to be followed are laid down in *Working Together to Safeguard Children* (1999). Where there is reasonable cause to suspect that a child may be suffering or is at risk of suffering significant harm, section 47 (9)(10)(11) places a duty on:

- any local authority;

- any local education authority;

- any housing authority;

- any health authority, special health authority, National Health Service Trust or Primary Care Trust; and

- any person authorised by the Secretary of State.

to help a local authority with its enquiries. In addition, the Police have a duty and a responsibility to investigate criminal offences committed against children.

> *Where a local authority –*
>
> *a. are informed that a child who lives, or is found in their area –*
>
> > *i   is the subject of an emergency protection order; or*
> > *ii   is in police protection; or*
>
> *b. have reasonable cause to suspect that a child who lives, or is found in their area is suffering, or is likely to suffer, significant harm,*
>
> *the authority shall make, or cause to be made, such enquiries as they consider necessary to enable them to decide whether they should take any action to safeguard or promote the child's welfare.*
>
> **Children Act 1989 s47(1)**

1.27   It is important to emphasise that the assessment should concentrate on the harm that has occurred or is likely to occur to the child as a result of child maltreatment, in order to inform future plans and the nature of services required. This is because there is substantial research evidence to suggest that the health and development of children, including their educational attainment, may be severely affected if they have been subjected to child maltreatment (Varma (ed), 1993; Adcock and White (eds), 1998; Jones and Ramchandani, 1999). It is not enough to have established the harm: action should be taken to safeguard and promote children's welfare. The duty to both safeguard and promote the child's welfare continues throughout the process of finding out whether there are grounds for concern that a child may be suffering or is at risk of suffering significant harm and deciding what action should be taken. Services may be provided to safeguard and promote the child's welfare (under Part III of the Act), while enquiries are being carried out, or, after protective action has been taken while an application is being made for a care or supervision order (under Part IV).

Providing Services

1.28   The local authority has a duty to respond to children in need in their area in the following ways:

- to provide services to children in need (s17);

- to provide such day care for children in need as appropriate (s18);

- to provide accommodation and maintenance to any child in need (s20 and s23);

- to advise, assist and befriend a child whilst he is being looked after and when he ceases to be looked after by the authority (s24);

- to provide services to minimise the effect of disabilities (Schedule 2, paragraph 6);

- to take steps to prevent neglect or ill-treatment (Schedule 2, paragraph 4);

- to take steps to encourage children not to commit criminal offences (Schedule 2, paragraph 7(b)); *and*

- to provide family centres (Schedule 2, paragraph 9).

1.29 The provision of services has a very broad meaning; the aim may be to prevent deterioration, that is to stop situations from getting worse, as well as to improve a child's health and development. Decisions about which services to provide should be based on an assessment of the child and families circumstances, in the following three domains: child's developmental needs, parenting capacity, and family and environmental factors. This framework for assessing children in need and their families is discussed fully in Chapter 2. It should be stressed that services, such as direct work with children and families, may be offered at the same time as family proceedings are in progress. The one does not preclude the other. **Furthermore, services may be provided to any members of the family in order to assist a child in need** (s17(3) of the Children Act 1989). The needs of parent carers are an integral part of an assessment. Providing services which meet the needs of parents is often the most effective means of promoting the welfare of children, in particular disabled children.

1.30 Services may include those provided by local authority children's services or by local authority adult services or by other agencies, on a single agency, inter-agency or multi-agency basis. By **inter-agency** it is meant that services are provided by individual agencies according to an agreed plan. By **multi-agency**, it is meant that services are provided by agencies acting in concert and drawing on pooled resources or a pooled budget or services defined as such in legislation, for example youth offending teams.

1.31 Services may be provided on a one off or episodic basis or over a longer period of time as determined by the child's plan (see paragraph 4.33). These provisions are often described as a **continuum of services** to support children and their families, and include care for a child in accommodation away from home. It is the function of Children's Services Planning to make sure this continuum of services is in place. Services provided in parallel with court proceedings or following on from a court order are provided under Part III of the Act.

1.32 In determining what services should be provided to a particular child and his family, social services departments are not charged with the same duty as the courts that the child's welfare shall be the 'paramount consideration' (s1(1)). Rather they have a broader duty to promote children's welfare to achieve the best possible outcomes for that particular child. Social services, in their assessment of whether a child is in need and how to respond to those needs, also have to take into consideration other children in the family and the general circumstances of that family. Social services have to identify the impact of what is happening to the child and also the likely impact of any intervention on that child and on other family members. Assessment requires careful consideration of the repercussions or consequences of providing specific types of services and the extent to which they will both safeguard and promote a particular child's welfare and development. This may be a complex equation which requires a high level of skill and professional judgement, involving all agency partners.

Principles Underpinning Assessment of Children in Need

1.33 Important principles underpin the approach to assessing children in need and their families which is outlined in this Guidance. They are important in understanding the development of the framework and in considering how an assessment should be carried out.

PRINCIPLES UNDERPINNING THE ASSESSMENT FRAMEWORK
Assessments:
- are child centred;
- are rooted in child development;
- are ecological in their approach;
- ensure equality of opportunity;
- involve working with children and families;
- build on strengths as well as identify difficulties;
- are inter-agency in their approach to assessment and the provision of services;
- are a continuing process, not a single event;
- are carried out in parallel with other action and providing services;
- are grounded in evidence based knowledge.

Child Centred

1.34 Fundamental to establishing whether a child is in need and how those needs should be best met is that the approach must be child centred. This means that the child is seen and kept in focus throughout the assessment and that account is always taken of the child's perspective. In complex situations where much is happening, attention can be diverted from the child to other issues which the family may be facing, such as a high level of conflict between adult family members, or depression being experienced by a parent or acute housing problems. This can result in the child becoming lost during assessment and the impact of the family and environmental circumstances on the child not being clearly identified and understood. The significance of seeing and observing the child throughout any assessment cannot be overstated.

1.35 The importance, therefore, of undertaking direct work with children during assessment is emphasised, including developing multiple, age, gender and culturally appropriate methods for ascertaining their wishes and feelings, and understanding the meaning of their experiences to them. Throughout the assessment process, the safety of the child should be ensured.

Rooted in Child Development

1.36 A thorough understanding of child development is critical to work with children and their families. Children have a range of different and complex developmental needs which must be met during different stages of childhood if optimal outcomes are to be achieved. Disabled children, including those with learning disabilities, may have a different rate of progress across the various developmental dimensions. Many disabled children will have quite individual patterns of development, for example a child with autism may acquire some skills ahead of the usual milestones but may never develop some communication skills. In addition, different aspects of development will have more or less weight at different stages of a child's life. For example, in the early years there is an emphasis on developing cognitive and language skills, achieving physical milestones and forming secure attachments; in middle childhood, social and educational development become more prominent; while the adolescent strives to reconcile the tensions between social and emotional dependence and independence.

1.37 Each child's development is significantly shaped by his or her particular experiences and the interaction between a series of factors. Some factors are intrinsic to individual children, such as characteristics of genetic inheritance or temperament. Other factors may include particular health problems or an impairment. Others may relate to their culture and to the physical and emotional environment in which a child is living.

1.38 Children referred for help are frequently very vulnerable and their opportunities to reach their full potential may have been or may be likely to be compromised in some way, for a variety of reasons. It is, therefore, crucial to know about the importance of developmental milestones which children need to reach, if they are to be healthy and achieve their full potential. This knowledge should recognise also that children are individuals and variations may occur in that sequence of development: such variations, however, may indicate services are necessary. Professionals should understand the consequences of variations for particular children of different ages, some of whom may have special educational needs and profound difficulties. Furthermore, they have to understand the significance of timing in a child's life. Children may not be getting what they require at a crucial stage in their development and time is passing. Plans and interventions should be based on a clear assessment of the developmental progress and difficulties a child may be experiencing and ensure that planned action is timely and appropriate in terms of the child's developmental needs.

Ecological Approach

1.39 An understanding of a child must be located within the context of the child's family (parents or caregivers and the wider family) and of the community and culture in which he or she is growing up. The significance of understanding the parent-child relationship has long been part of child welfare practice: less so the importance of the interface between environmental factors and a child's development, and the influence of these environmental factors on parents' capacities to respond to their child's needs (Jack, 1997; Stevenson, 1998 and others). The association between economic disadvantage and the chances that children will fail to thrive (Utting, 1995) and the association between a teenager's friendship group and pro-social and anti-social behaviour (Rutter *et al*, 1998) are well researched. So is the impact on parenting capacity of a supportive wider family or of struggling to bring up children in impoverished living conditions. 'Living on a low income in a run down neighbourhood does not make it impossible to be the affectionate, authoritative parent of healthy, sociable children. But it does, undeniably, make it more difficult' (Utting, 1995, p. 40).

1.40 **Assessment, therefore, should take account of three domains:**

- **the child's developmental needs;**

- **the parents' or caregivers' capacities to respond appropriately;**

- **the wider family and environmental factors.**

1.41 The interaction between the three domains and the way they influence each other must be carefully analysed in order to gain a complete picture of a child's unmet needs and how to identify the best response to them.

Ensuring Equality of Opportunity

1.42 The Children Act 1989 is built on the premise that 'children and young people and their parents should all be considered as individuals with particular needs and potentialities' (Department of Health, 1989), that differences in bringing up children due to family structures, religion, culture and ethnic origins should be respected and understood and that those children with 'specific social needs arising out of disability or a health condition' have their assessed needs met and reviewed (Department of Health, 1998a). Ensuring that all children who are assessed as in need have the opportunity to achieve optimal development, according to their circumstances and age, is an important principle. Furthermore, since discrimination of all kinds is an everyday reality in many children's lives, every effort must be made to ensure that agencies' responses do not reflect or reinforce that experience and indeed, should counteract it. Some vulnerable children may have been particularly disadvantaged in their access to important opportunities, such as those who have suffered multiple family disruptions or prolonged maltreatment by abuse or neglect and are subsequently looked by the local authority. Their health and educational needs will require particular attention in order to optimise their long term outcomes in young adulthood.

1.43 Ensuring equality of opportunity does not mean that all children are treated the same. It does mean understanding and working sensitively and knowledgeably with diversity to identify the particular issues for a child and his/her family, taking account of experiences and family context. This is further elaborated in the chapters in the accompanying practice guidance on working with disabled children and with black children.

Working with Children and their Families

1.44 The majority of parents want to do the best for their children. Whatever their circumstances or difficulties, the concept of partnership between the State and the family, in situations where families are in need of assistance in bringing up their children, lies at the heart of child care legislation. The importance of partnership has been further reinforced by a substantial number of research findings, including the child protection studies (Department of Health, 1995d) and family support studies (Butt and Box,

1998; Aldgate and Bradley, 1999; Tunstill and Aldgate, 2000). In the process of finding out what is happening to a child, it will be critical to develop a co-operative working relationship, so that parents or caregivers feel respected and informed, that staff are being open and honest with them, and that they in turn are confident about providing vital information about their child, themselves and their circumstances.

1.45 Working with family members is not an end in itself; the objective must always be to safeguard and promote the welfare of the child. The child, therefore, must be kept in focus. It requires sensitivity to and understanding of the circumstances of families and their particular needs, for example where English is not a parent's first language or where adults who are significant to a child are not living in the same household or where a parent is disabled or mentally ill. For a disabled parent reasonable adjustments will be needed, for example, it may be necessary to provide information to a blind parent in an alternative format such as Braille or on audio tape, or to communicate with a deaf parent using British Sign Language.

1.46 Parents value taking part in discussions about how and where the assessment will be carried out, as well as what they hope it will achieve. Similarly, according to the age and development of the child, listening to what children have to say and working openly and honestly is valued by them and produces more effective outcomes. This is discussed further in Chapter 3.

1.47 Developing a working relationship with children and family members will not always be easy to achieve and can be difficult especially when there have been concerns about significant harm to the child. However resistant the family or difficult the circumstances, it remains important to continue to try to find ways of engaging the family in the assessment process. Use of mediation may be helpful in assisting professionals and family members to work together. The quality of the early or initial contact will affect later working relationships and the ability of professionals to secure an agreed understanding of what is happening and to provide help. Studies have found that even in situations where child sexual abuse is alleged, despite early difficulties that may arise because of having to take immediate child protective action, it may still be possible to work with children and their parents (Cleaver and Freeman, 1995; Jones and Ramchandani, 1999). Working with children and family members, where there are concerns about a child suffering significant harm is discussed in paragraphs 7.2 to 7.12 in *Working Together to Safeguard Children* (1999).

Building on Strengths as well as Identifying Difficulties

1.48 It is important that an approach to assessment, which is based on a full understanding of what is happening to a child in the context of his or her family and the wider community, examines carefully the nature of the interactions between the child, family and environmental factors and identifies both positive and negative influences. These will vary for each child. Nothing can be assumed; the facts must be sought, the meaning attached to them explored and weighed up with the family. Sometimes assessments have been largely in terms of a child or family's difficulties or problems, or the risks seen to be attached to particular behaviours or situations. What is working well or what may be acting as positive factors for the child and family may be overlooked. For example, a single mother, in crisis over health, financial and housing problems, may still be managing to get her child up in time in the mornings, washed, dressed, breakfasted and off to school each day. An older child, living in a family periodically disrupted by domestic violence, may be provided with welcome respite care on a regular basis by a grandmother living locally. Working with a child or family's strengths may be an important part of a plan to resolve difficulties.

1.49   This is not to suggest that staff should suspend their critical professional judgement and adopt a 'rule of optimism' (Dingwall et al, 1983). It is important, however, that they not only identify the deficits in assessing a family's situation, but also make a realistic and informed appraisal of the strengths and resources in the family and the relative weight that should be given to each. These can be mobilised to safeguard and promote the child's welfare.

Inter-Agency Approach to Assessment and Provision of Services

1.50   From birth, all children will become involved with a variety of different agencies in the community, particularly in relation to their health, day care and educational development. A range of professionals, including midwives, health visitors, general practitioners, nursery staff and teachers, will have a role in assessing their general wellbeing and development. Children who are vulnerable are, therefore, likely to be identified by these professionals, who will have an important responsibility in deciding whether to refer them to social services for further assessment and help. The knowledge they already have about a child and family is an essential component of any assessment. These agencies may also be required to provide more specialist assessment for those smaller numbers of children where there are particular causes for concern. Similarly, responding to the needs of vulnerable children may require services from agencies other than social services or in combination with social services help. Inter-agency work starts as soon as there are concerns about a child's welfare, not just when there is an enquiry about significant harm. An important underlying principle of the approach to assessment in this Guidance, therefore, is that it is based on a inter-agency model in which it is not just social services departments which are the assessors and providers of services.

A Continuing Process, not a Single Event

1.51   Understanding what is happening to a vulnerable child within the context of his or her family and the local community cannot be achieved as a single event. It must necessarily be a process of gathering information from a variety of sources and making sense of it with the family and, very often, with several professionals concerned with the child's welfare.

1.52   This assessment process involves one or more of the following:

- establishing good working relationships with the child and family;

- developing a deeper understanding through multiple approaches to the assessment task;

- setting up joint or parallel assessment arrangements with other professionals and agencies, as appropriate;

- determining which types of intervention are most likely to be effective for which needs.

1.53   For many children who come to the attention of social services departments, the process will be relatively straightforward and short term. The more complex or serious a child's situation, however, the more time it may take to understand thoroughly what is happening to the child, the reasons why and the impact on the child and the more it is also likely to involve several agencies in that process. Where there are concerns about a child's safety, decisions to safeguard the child may have to be made quickly pending greater understanding of the child's circumstances. Once it has been established whether a child is in need, further questions will remain to be answered about:

- the parents' views of the child's needs and services required;

- the precise nature of these needs;

- the reasons for them;

- the priority for action and/or resources;

- the potential for change in the child and family;

- the best options to be pursued;

- the child's and family's response to intervention;

- how well the child is doing.

Assessment should continue throughout a period of intervention, and intervention may start at the beginning of an assessment.

1.54   Assessment is thus an iterative process which for some children will continue throughout work with the child and the family or caregivers. In order to achieve the best outcomes, the framework should be used also at important decision making times when reviewing the child's progress and future plans. Use of the Assessment Framework linked to the Looking After Children materials which have been used to monitor the child's progress whilst they have been looked after will enhance care planning and reviewing processes. This will provide an integrated framework for children looked after which should be used at key decision making points including return home from residential or foster care, or longer term plans for an alternative family placement such as adoption, or when leaving care.

1.55   This does not mean that assessment should be over intrusive, repeated unnecessarily or continued without any clear purpose or outcome. Effective discrimination between different types and levels of need are key considerations.

Action and Services are Provided in Parallel with Assessment

1.56   Although assessment is generally described in this Guidance as a discrete process which will result in an understanding of need, from which a plan of action and intervention can be developed, in many situations there is inevitably overlap between these different activities. Undertaking an assessment with a family can begin a process of understanding and change by key family members. A practitioner may, during the process of gathering information, be instrumental in bringing about change by the questions asked, by listening to members of the family, by validating the family's difficulties or concerns, and by providing information and advice. The process of assessment should be therapeutic in itself. This does not preclude taking timely action either to provide immediate services or to take steps to protect a child who is suffering or is likely to suffer significant harm. Action and services should be provided according to the needs of the child and family, in parallel with assessment where necessary, and not await completion of the assessment.

Grounded in Evidence

1.57 Each professional discipline derives its knowledge from a particular theoretical base, related research findings and accumulated practice wisdom and experience. Social work practice, however, differs in that it derives its knowledge from theory and research in many different disciplines. Practice is also based on policies laid down in legislation and government guidance. It is essential that practitioners and their managers ensure that practice and its supervision are grounded in the most up to date knowledge and that they make use of the resources described in the practice guidance as well as other critical materials, including:

- relevant research findings;

- national and local statistical data;

- national policy and practice guidance;

- Social Services Inspectorate Inspection Standards;

- Government and local inspection, audit and performance assessment reports;

- lessons learnt from national and local inquiries and reviews of cases of child maltreatment.

1.58 Practice is expected to be evidence based, by which it is meant that practitioners:

- use knowledge critically from research and practice about the needs of children and families and the outcomes of services and interventions to inform their assessment and planning;

- record and update information systematically, distinguishing sources of information, for example direct observation, other agency records or interviews with family members;

- learn from the views of users of services ie. children and families;

- valuate continously whether the intervention is effective in responding to the needs of an individual child and family and modifying their interventions accordingly;

- evaluate rigorously the information, processes and outcomes from the practitioner's own interventions to develop practice wisdom.

1.59 The combination of evidence based practice grounded in knowledge with finely balanced professional judgement is the foundation for effective practice with children and families.

1.60 The knowledge base from which these principles are derived and the application of the principles to the process of assessing children in need and their families are developed in subsequent chapters.

2

Framework for the Assessment of Children in Need

Framework for the Assessment of Children in Need

2.1 Assessing whether a child is in need and the nature of these needs requires a systematic approach which uses the same framework or conceptual map for gathering and analysing information about all children and their families, but discriminates effectively between different types and levels of need. The framework in this guidance is developed from the legislative foundations and principles in Chapter 1 and an extensive research and practice knowledge which is outlined in the practice guidance (Department of Health, 2000a). It requires a thorough understanding of:

- the developmental needs of children;

- the capacities of parents or caregivers to respond appropriately to those needs;

- the impact of wider family and environmental factors on parenting capacity and children.

2.2 These are described as three inter-related systems or domains, each of which has a number of critical dimensions (Figure 2). The interaction or the influence of these dimensions on each other requires careful exploration during assessment, with the ultimate aim being to understand how they affect the child or children in the family.

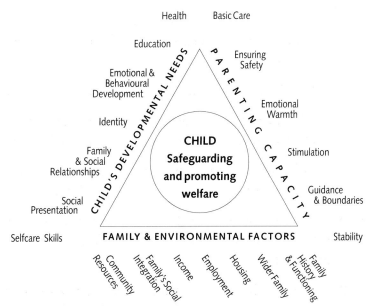

Figure 2 **The Assessment Framework (the above diagram has been reproduced at Appendix A for ease of photocopying)**

This analysis of the child's situation will inform planning and action to secure the best outcomes for the child. The Assessment Framework can be represented in the form of a triangle or pyramid, with the child's welfare at the centre. This emphasises that all assessment activity and subsequent planning and provision of services must focus on ensuring that the child's welfare is safeguarded and promoted.

Dimensions of a Child's Developmental Needs

2.3   Assessment of what is happening to a child requires that each aspect of a child's developmental progress is examined, in the context of the child's age and stage of development. This includes knowing whether a child has reached his or her expected developmental milestones. Account must be taken of any particular vulnerabilities, such as a learning disability or a physically impairing condition, and the impact they may be having on progress in any of the developmental dimensions. Consideration should also be given to the socially and environmentally disabling factors which have an impact on a child's development, such as limited access for those who are disabled and other forms of discrimination. Children who have been maltreated may suffer impairment to their development as a result of injuries sustained and/or the impact of the trauma caused by their abuse. There must be a clear understanding of what a particular child is capable of achieving successfully at each stage of development, in order to ensure that he or she has the opportunity to achieve his or her full potential.

2.4   The child's developmental dimensions are described on page 19. These descriptions are intended to be **illustrative** rather than comprehensive of the different components of each dimension.

2.5   The child development dimensions have been taken from the work of Roy Parker and colleagues which was commissioned by the Department of Health (1991) to find practical measures to assess the progress of children accommodated in children's homes and foster care, and to improve their outcomes. During the development stages of that work, the materials were tested with a large number of families in the community and it was found 'that the Assessment and Action Records can be used with parents and children in the community as a means of identifying difficulties and discussing how to address them' (Ward, 1995). These dimensions have therefore been demonstrated to be salient for all children.

2.6   When practitioners are undertaking an assessment of a child's developmental needs, they should:

- identify the developmental areas to be covered and recorded;

- plan how developmental progress is to be measured;

- ensure proper account is taken of a child's age and stage of development;

- analyse information as the basis for planning future action.

2.7   A number of questionnaires and scales have been assembled concurrently with the development of this guidance to assist social services staff, in particular, in specific areas when undertaking child and family assessments. Eight have been published in The Family Pack of Questionnaires and Scales (Department of Health, Cox and Bentovim, 2000) and a further two, the *Home Inventory* (Caldwell and Bradley, 1984)

DIMENSIONS OF CHILD'S DEVELOPMENTAL NEEDS

Health

Includes growth and development as well as physical and mental wellbeing. The impact of genetic factors and of any impairment should be considered. Involves receiving appropriate health care when ill, an adequate and nutritious diet, exercise, immunisations where appropriate and developmental checks, dental and optical care and, for older children, appropriate advice and information on issues that have an impact on health, including sex education and substance misuse.

Education

Covers all areas of a child's cognitive development which begins from birth. *Includes* opportunities: for play and interaction with other children; to have access to books; to acquire a range of skills and interests; to experience success and achievement. Involves an adult interested in educational activities, progress and achievements, who takes account of the child's starting point and any special educational needs.

Emotional and Behavioural Development

Concerns the appropriateness of response demonstrated in feelings and actions by a child, initially to parents and caregivers and, as the child grows older, to others beyond the family.
Includes nature and quality of early attachments, characteristics of temperament, adaptation to change, response to stress and degree of appropriate self control.

Identity

Concerns the child's growing sense of self as a separate and valued person. *Includes* the child's view of self and abilities, self image and self esteem, and having a positive sense of individuality. Race, religion, age, gender, sexuality and disability may all contribute to this. Feelings of belonging and acceptance by family, peer group and wider society, including other cultural groups.

Family and Social Relationships

Development of empathy and the capacity to place self in someone else's shoes. *Includes* a stable and affectionate relationship with parents or caregivers, good relationships with siblings, increasing importance of age appropriate friendships with peers and other significant persons in the child's life and response of family to these relationships.

Social Presentation

Concerns child's growing understanding of the way in which appearance, behaviour, and any impairment are perceived by the outside world and the impression being created.
Includes appropriateness of dress for age, gender, culture and religion; cleanliness and personal hygiene; and availability of advice from parents or caregivers about presentation in different settings.

Self Care Skills

Concerns the acquisition by a child of practical, emotional and communication competencies required for increasing independence. Includes early practical skills of dressing and feeding, opportunities to gain confidence and practical skills to undertake activities away from the family and independent living skills as older children. *Includes* encouragement to acquire social problem solving approaches. Special attention should be given to the impact of a child's impairment and other vulnerabilities, and on social circumstances affecting these in the development of self care skills.

and the *Assessment of Family Competence, Strengths and Difficulties* developed by Bentovim and Bingley Miller (forthcoming) will be published later this year. In addition there are others which may be of use to assist the process of assessment.

2.8 Use of questionnaires and scales enables children and caregivers to express their views about their particular circumstances. They have been found also to identify areas of concern or difficulty which have not been identified previously through interviews or observations.

Dimensions of Parenting Capacity

2.9 Critically important to a child's health and development is the ability of parents or caregivers to ensure that the child's developmental needs are being appropriately and adequately responded to, and to adapt to his or her changing needs over time. The parenting tasks are described on page 21. Again, these descriptions are illustrative rather than comprehensive of all parenting tasks.

2.10 It is important that parenting capacity be considered in the context of the family's structure and functioning, and who contributes to the parental care of the child (see Family and Environmental Factors, paragraphs 2.13 to 2.25).

2.11 In family situations where there is cause for concern about what is happening to a child, it becomes even more important to gather information about how these tasks are being carried out by each parent or caregiver in terms of:

- their response to a child and his or her behaviour or circumstances;

- the manner in which they are responding to the child's needs and the areas where they are experiencing difficulties in meeting needs or failing to do so;

- the effect this child has on them;

- the quality of the parent – child relationship;

- their understanding of the child's needs and development;

- their comprehension of parenting tasks and the relevance of these to the child's developmental needs;

- the impact of any difficulties they may be experiencing themselves on their ability to carry out parental tasks and responsibilities (distinguishing realisation from aspiration);

- the impact of past experiences on their current parenting capacity;

- their ability to face and accept their difficulties;

- their ability to use support and accept help;

- their capacity for adaptation and change in their parenting response.

Observation of interactions is as critically important as the way they are described by the adults involved.

2.12 The parenting tasks undertaken by fathers or father figures should be addressed alongside those of mothers or mother figures. In some families, a single parent may be

DIMENSIONS OF PARENTING CAPACITY

Basic Care

Providing for the child's physical needs, and appropriate medical and dental care.
Includes provision of food, drink, warmth, shelter, clean and appropriate clothing and adequate personal hygiene.

Ensuring Safety

Ensuring the child is adequately protected from harm or danger.
Includes protection from significant harm or danger, and from contact with unsafe adults/other children and from self-harm. Recognition of hazards and danger both in the home and elsewhere.

Emotional Warmth

Ensuring the child's emotional needs are met and giving the child a sense of being specially valued and a positive sense of own racial and cultural identity.
Includes ensuring the child's requirements for secure, stable and affectionate relationships with significant adults, with appropriate sensitivity and responsiveness to the child's needs. Appropriate physical contact, comfort and cuddling sufficient to demonstrate warm regard, praise and encouragement.

Stimulation

Promoting child's learning and intellectual development through encouragement and cognitive stimulation and promoting social opportunities.
Includes facilitating the child's cognitive development and potential through interaction, communication, talking and responding to the child's language and questions, encouraging and joining the child's play, and promoting educational opportunities. Enabling the child to experience success and ensuring school attendance or equivalent opportunity. Facilitating child to meet challenges of life.

Guidance and Boundaries

Enabling the child to regulate their own emotions and behaviour.
The key parental tasks are *demonstrating and modelling* appropriate behaviour and control of emotions and interactions with others, and *guidance* which involves setting boundaries, so that the child is able to develop an internal model of moral values and conscience, and social behaviour appropriate for the society within which they will grow up. The aim is to enable the child to grow into an autonomous adult, holding their own values, and able to demonstrate appropriate behaviour with others rather than having to be dependent on rules outside themselves. This includes not over protecting children from exploratory and learning experiences.
Includes social problem solving, anger management, consideration for others, and effective discipline and shaping of behaviour.

Stability

Providing a sufficiently stable family environment to enable a child to develop and maintain a secure attachment to the primary caregiver(s) in order to ensure optimal development.
Includes: ensuring secure attachments are not disrupted, providing consistency of emotional warmth over time and responding in a similar manner to the same behaviour. Parental responses change and develop according to child's developmental progress. In addition, ensuring children keep in contact with important family members and significant others.

performing most or all of the parenting tasks. In others, there may be a number of important caregivers in a child's life, each playing a different part which may have positive or negative consequences. A wide range of adults, for example grandparents, step relations, child minders or baby sitters, may have a significant role in caring for a child. A distinction has to be clearly made between the contribution of each parent or caregiver to a child's wellbeing and development. Where a child has suffered significant harm, it is particularly important to distinguish between the capabilities of the abusing parent and the potentially protective parent. This information can also contribute to an understanding of the impact the parents' relationship with each other may have on their respective capacities to respond appropriately to their child's needs. The quality of the inter-parental relationship, which has an impact on the child's wellbeing will be considered more explicitly in the following section on family and environmental factors.

Family and Environmental Factors

2.13　The care and upbringing of children does not take place in a vacuum. All family members are influenced both positively and negatively by the wider family, the neighbourhood and social networks in which they live. The history of the child's family and of individual family members may have a significant impact on the child and parents. Some family members, for example, may have grown up in a completely different environment to the child, others may have had to leave their country of origin because of war or other adverse conditions, and others may have experienced abuse and neglect as children.

2.14　The narration and impact of family histories and experiences can play an important part in understanding what is happening currently to a family. An adult's capacity to parent may be crucially related to his or her childhood experiences of family life and past adult experiences prior to the current difficulties. The family may be in transition, for example refugee families.

2.15　An understanding of how the family usually functions, and how it functions when under stress can be very helpful in identifying what factors may assist parents in carrying out their parenting roles. Of particular importance is the quality and nature of the relationship between a child's parents and how this affects the child. For example, sustained conflict between parents is detrimental to children's welfare. The quality of relationships between siblings may also be of major significance to a child's welfare. Account must be taken of the diversity of family styles and structures, particularly who counts as family and who is important to the child.

2.16　The impact of multiple caregivers will need careful exploration, with an understanding of the context in which the care is being provided. As Cleaver (Department of Health and Cleaver, 2000) writes in the notes of guidance for use with the assessment records:

> Children can be protected from the adverse consequences of parenting problems when someone else meets the child's developmental needs.

She adds that it is important to record when there is evidence that no one is responding appropriately to the child. In some circumstances children who have a number of caregivers may be more vulnerable to being maltreated. Special attention should be given to the needs of disabled children who experience multiple caregivers as part of their regular routine, and to their need for reasonable continuity of caregivers.

FAMILY AND ENVIRONMENTAL FACTORS

Family History and Functioning

Family history includes both genetic and psycho-social factors.

Family functioning is influenced by who is living in the household and how they are related to the child; significant changes in family/household composition; history of childhood experiences of parents; chronology of significant life events and their meaning to family members; nature of family functioning, including sibling relationships and its impact on the child; parental strengths and difficulties, including those of an absent parent; the relationship between separated parents.

Wider Family

Who are considered to be members of the wider family by the child and the parents?

Includes related and non-related persons and absent wider family. What is their role and importance to the child and parents and in precisely what way?

Housing

Does the accommodation have basic amenities and facilities appropriate to the age and development of the child and other resident members? Is the housing accessible and suitable to the needs of disabled family members?

Includes the interior and exterior of the accommodation and immediate surroundings. Basic amenities include water, heating, sanitation, cooking facilities, sleeping arrangements and cleanliness, hygiene and safety and their impact on the child's upbringing.

Employment

Who is working in the household, their pattern of work and any changes? What impact does this have on the child? How is work or absence of work viewed by family members? How does it affect their relationship with the child?

Includes children's experience of work and its impact on them.

Income

Income available over a sustained period of time. Is the family in receipt of all its benefit entitlements? Sufficiency of income to meet the family's needs. The way resources available to the family are used. Are there financial difficulties which affect the child?

Family's Social Integration

Exploration of the wider context of the local neighbourhood and community and its impact on the child and parents.

Includes the degree of the family's integration or isolation, their peer groups, friendship and social networks and the importance attached to them.

Community Resources

Describes all facilities and services in a neighbourhood, including universal services of primary health care, day care and schools, places of worship, transport, shops and leisure activities.

Includes availability, accessibility and standard of resources and impact on the family, including disabled members.

2.17 In families where a parent is not living in the same household as the child, it is important to identify what role that parent has in the child's life and the significance to the child of the relationship with that parent. It cannot be assumed that parents who live apart are estranged. This arrangement may be by mutual agreement.

2.18 A wide range of environmental factors can either help or hinder the family's functioning. Here it is important to think broadly and creatively about the family and environmental factors described on the previous page.

2.19 Careful account should be taken of how these factors are influencing both a child's progress and the parents' responses. This can be illustrated by the following examples of the inter-relationship between such factors and a child's development:

- **Family history**
  A child may have a genetic condition or pre-disposition, such as sickle cell disorder or Huntington's Chorea, which may affect current or future physical or mental health and the need for services.

- **Family Functioning**
  Despite a recent separation, the parents co-operate regarding decisions about key events in a 10 year old boy's life such that he continues to attend the same school, maintains a strong group of friends, and is fully supported in his education by both parents. This enables him to do well in school.

- **Wider family**
  A child may have developed a close, affectionate attachment to a friend's parent who, over a number of years, compensates for chronic parental problems in the family home, giving that child a sense of belonging and selfesteem. This may become a resource to be mobilised at the time of family breakdown.

- **Housing**
  Accommodation which is damp, infested and overcrowded may be contributing to a low birth weight baby's failure to thrive and chronic ear, nose and chest problems, requiring urgent action.

- **Employment**
  The expectation that a 13 year old girl will assist regularly in the family business may result in her sudden failure to keep up with school work and difficult behaviour in class.

- **Income**
  A low income over many years and parents' inability to manage on this income may mean a young adolescent being bullied at school simply because he is wearing clothes which do not have the correct designer logo.

- **Family's social integration**
  Constant racial harassment and bullying in a neighbourhood may result in a teenager from a minority ethnic family being isolated and excluded from positive and affirming friendship group experiences at a formative stage of developing his identity.

- **Access to community resources**
  Knowledge of resources available in the community which are accessible and accommodate disabled children may enable an isolated single mother to organise

out of school care and activities for her 6 year old disabled child, thus enabling her to remain in work.

2.20 The complex interplay of factors across all three domains should be carefully understood and analysed. Parents may be experiencing their own problems which may have an impact through their behaviour on their capacity to respond to their child's needs. This could cover a variety of situations. It could include parents who are unable to read or write and are therefore unable to respond to notes sent home from school. On the other hand, it could include a child being traumatised by witnessing her mother being regularly assaulted by her father.

2.21 The publication *Children's Needs – Parenting Capacity* by Cleaver et al (1999) focuses on the impact of particular parental problems (mental illness, domestic violence, drug and alcohol misuse) on a child's development while *Crossing Bridges* (Falkov (ed) 1998) addresses parental mental illnesses in more detail. Such problems may adversely affect a parent's ability to respond to the needs of his or her child. While some children grow up apparently unscathed, others exhibit emotional and behavioural disorders as a result of these childhood experiences. This knowledge can assist professionals to be clear about the impact of a parent's difficulties on a child. In some situations, where the parents' problems are severe, such as major psychiatric illness or substance misuse, there may need to be **joint** or **concurrent assessments**; to examine the parent's problems, the impact of those problems on the child, and the effect of the child on the parent. Such assessments should be carried out within a clear focus on the needs of the child.

2.22 There is increasing knowledge about the characteristics of adults who maltreat children. Research has shown a strong association between domestic violence and child abuse. It has shown also, that not all parents who have suffered childhood abuse or deprivation go on to maltreat their children, but a significant proportion of parents who harm their children have been abused themselves (Department of Health, 1995d).

2.23 The interactions between different factors are often not straightforward which is why it is important that:

- information is gathered and recorded systematically with care and precision;

- information is checked and discussed with parents and, where appropriate, with the child;

- differences in views about information and its importance are clearly recorded;

- the strengths and difficulties **within** families are assessed and understood;

- the vulnerabilities and protective factors in the child's world are examined;

- the impact of what is happening on the child is clearly identified.

Chapter 4 elaborates on the processes of analysis, judgement and decision making which follow on from the information gathering and collation stages.

2.24 Ward (1995, p.85) in her community study of almost 400 children and their families concludes:

It is likely to be the interaction between a number of factors rather than any specific characteristic that leads to parenting difficulties. Thus most families are able to overcome adversities and provide their children with a sufficiently nurturing environment, although they may fall down in one or two areas. Only a very small proportion are unable to provide a sufficiently consistent standard of care across all seven (child development) dimensions, but it is they who form the group whose children are most likely to be admitted to care or accommodation.

2.25 The framework for assessment is, therefore, a conceptual map which can be used to understand what is happening to all children in whatever circumstances they may be growing up. For most children referred or whose families seek help, the issues of concern will be relatively straightforward, parents will be clear about requiring assistance and the impact on the child will not be difficult to identify. For a smaller number of children, the causes for concern will be serious and complex and the relationship between their needs, their parents' responses and the circumstances in which they are living, less straightforward. In these situations, further, more detailed and, in some cases, specialist assessment will be required. These issues are considered in the next chapter on the process of assessment.

Inclusive Practice

2.26 The Assessment Framework is predicated on the principle that children are children first, whatever may distinguish some children from others. This poses a challenge for staff - how to develop inclusive practice which recognises that all children share the same developmental needs to reach their optimal potential but that the rate or pattern of progress of individual children may vary because of factors associated with health and impairment. At the same time, due weight needs to be given to other important influences on children's development. Prominent amongst these are genetic factors, the quality of attachment to primary caregivers and the quality of everyday life experiences.

2.27 When assessing a child's needs and circumstances, care has to be taken to ensure that issues which fundamentally shape children's identity and wellbeing, their progress and outcomes are fully understood and incorporated into the framework for assessment. Dutt and Phillips (Department of Health, 2000a) write:

> Issues of race and culture cannot be added to a list for separate consideration during an assessment, they are integral to the assessment process. From referral through to core assessment, intervention and planning, race and culture have to be taken account of using an holistic framework for assessment.

2.28 In assessing the needs of children, practitioners have to take account of diversity in children, understand its origins and pay careful attention to its impact on a child's development and the interaction with parental responses and wider family and environmental factors.

2.29 Use of the framework requires that children and families' differences must be approached with knowledge and sensitivity in a non-judgemental way. Ignorance can result in stereotyping and in inappropriate or even damaging assumptions being made, resulting in a lack of accuracy and balance in analysing children's needs. To achieve sensitive and inclusive practice, staff should **avoid**:

- using one set of cultural assumptions and stereotypes to understand the child and family's circumstances;

- insensitivity to racial and cultural variations within groups and between individuals;

- making unreasoned assumptions without evidence;

- failing to take account of experiences of any discrimination in an individual's response to public services;

- failing to take account of the barriers which prevent the social integration of families with disabled members;

- attaching meaning to information without confirming the interpretation with the child and family members.

2.30 The use of the framework, derived from children's developmental needs and which also takes account of the context in which they are growing up, takes on more significance in relation to children for whom discrimination is likely to be part of their life experience. Such children and their families may suffer subsequent disadvantage and a failure of access to appropriate services. It is for this reason that chapters have been included in the practice guidance which consider in more detail issues of race and culture and of disability in assessing the needs of children in the context of their family and their environment.

Disability Discrimination Act 1995

2.31 Under Part III of the Disability Discrimination Act 1995 (rights of access to goods, facilities and services) service providers, including social services departments and health but not as yet education, must not discriminate against disabled people (including children) by refusing to provide any service which is provided to members of the public, by providing a lower standard of service or offering a service on less favourable terms. These requirements came into force on 2 December 1996.

2.32 Since October 1999, service providers have had to take reasonable steps to:

- change any policy, practice or procedure which makes it impossible or unreasonably difficult for disabled people to make use of services;

- provide an auxiliary aid or service if it would enable (or make easier for) disabled people to make use of services; and

- provide a reasonable alternative method of making services available to disabled people where a physical feature makes it impossible or unreasonably difficult for disabled people to make use of them.

2.33 From 2004 service providers will have to take reasonable steps to remove, alter or provide reasonable means of avoiding physical features that make it impossible or unreasonably difficult for disabled people to use the services.

3

The Process of Assessing Children in Need

Process of Assessment and Timing

3.1 Assessment is the first stage in helping a vulnerable child and his or her family, its purpose being 'to contribute to the understanding necessary for appropriate planning' (Compton and Galaway, 1989) and action. Assessment has several phases which overlap and lead into planning, action and review:

- clarification of source of referral and reason;

- acquisition of information;

- exploring facts and feelings;

- giving meaning to the situation which distinguishes the child and family's understanding and feelings from those of the professionals;

- reaching an understanding of what is happening, problems, strengths and difficulties, and the impact on the child (with the family wherever possible);

- drawing up an analysis of the needs of the child and parenting capacity within their family and community context as a basis for formulating a plan.

3.2 Prior to social services departments becoming involved with a child and family, a number of other agencies and community based groups may have had contact with the family. For some children, assessments will have already been carried out for purposes other than determining whether they are a child in need. In particular, health and education will have undertaken routine assessments as part of monitoring children's developmental progress. The familiarity of other agencies with the Assessment Framework will assist when making a referral to a social services department or contributing to an assessment of a child in need, thereby facilitating a common understanding of the child's needs within their family context.

3.3 The response from social services departments to an initial contact or a referral requesting help is critically important. At that point the foundation is laid for future work with the child or family. Children and families may have contact with social services staff in a wide range of settings. These may be as diverse as a family or day centre, a social services area office, an accident and emergency, adult or paediatric unit in a hospital, an education setting, an adolescent drop-in service or specialist services for adults. Not all staff in these settings will be professionals or qualified in work with children and families. This will apply particularly to those who work predominantly with adults. Whoever has first contact with a child or family member, however, has a vital role in influencing the course of future work. It is quite clear from research that the quality of the early or initial contact affects later working relationships with professionals. Furthermore, recording of information about the initial contact or referral contributes to the first phase of assessment. It is essential, therefore, that all staff responding to families or to referrers are familiar with the principles which underpin the Assessment Framework and are aware of the importance of the information collected and recorded at this stage.

3.4 For unqualified or inexperienced staff, the NSPCC chart *Referrals Involving A Child* (Cleaver *et al*, 1998) may act as a useful aide memoire to ensure that important information, which will assist later decision making, is not overlooked. It should not be treated as a check list but, used alongside local agency referral forms, it can serve as a reminder of:

- issues which may need to be covered in a response to the referrer;

- matters raised by the referrer that should be recorded.

The chart is included in Appendix C.

3.5 Arrangements for managing the reception of initial contacts or referrals vary widely according to local circumstances. It is important that social services for adults are aware of their responsibilities to children of adults who have parenting responsibilities and ensure that an initial assessment takes place to ascertain whether the children are children in need under s17 of the Children Act 1989 (Department of Health, forthcoming, a).

3.6 It is important also that each social services department has structures and systems in place to ensure an effective, accessible and speedy response to children and families. Some local authorities are developing innovative approaches to referrals and initial assessment. These include local telephone help lines, help desks, multi-agency information and advice centres and drop-in services. An example of this is the help desk service established in a rural county below (Figure 3). When there are such arrangements, it becomes imperative that reception staff are carefully selected and

FEATURES:
- one accessible, responsive point of contact in a district for child and family referrals.
- staffed by a team of specially selected and trained unqualified referral and information co-ordinators, administrative reception staff, qualified social workers (to undertake assessments of children whose welfare may need safeguarding and promoting) and a team manager.
- priority to provide a safe short term service at the front end through:
  - advice and advocacy eg. welfare benefits
  - information
  - help eg. by signposting
  - referral taking by telephone and personal interview
  - initial and core assessments of children in need
  - direct access to practical services

Figure 3 **Helpdesk for Children's Services in a Rural County**

trained for their tasks. Reception staff will also need the support of qualified practitioners and managers to ensure that situations of serious or immediate concern about a child receive prompt and expert professional attention.

3.7 Time, as discussed in Chapter 1, is critical in a child's life. A timely response to responding to a child's needs means that the process of assessment cannot continue unchecked over a prolonged period without an analysis being made of what is happening and what action is needed, however difficult or complex the child's circumstances. Prior to the publication of the Government's Objectives for children's social services (Department of Health, 1999e), no timescales had been set for completing assessments of children in need, although there had been timescales for action to be taken to protect children where there were concerns that a child was suffering or likely to suffer significant harm. This has now been remedied and timescales have been specified in the objectives for children's social services.

3.8 There is an expectation that **within one working day** of a referral being received or new information coming to or from within a social services department about an open case, there will be a decision about what response is required. A referral is defined as a request for services to be provided by the social services department. The response may include no action, but that is itself a decision and should be made promptly and recorded. The referrer should be informed of the decision and its rationale, as well as the parents or caregivers and the child, if appropriate.

3.9 A decision to gather more information constitutes an initial assessment. An initial assessment is defined as a brief assessment of each child referred to social services with a request for services to be provided. This should be undertaken **within a maximum of 7 working days** but could be very brief depending on the child's circumstances. It should address the dimensions of the Assessment Framework, determining whether the child is in need, the nature of any services required, from where and within what timescales, and whether a further, more detailed core assessment should be undertaken. An initial assessment is deemed to have commenced at the point of referral to the social services department or when new information on an open case indicates an initial assessment should be repeated. All staff responding to referrals and undertaking initial assessments should address the dimensions which constitute the Assessment Framework. There is more detailed discussion about the contribution of respective agencies in Chapter 5.

3.10 Depending on the child's circumstances, an initial assessment may include some or all of the following:

- interviews with child and family members, as appropriate;
- involvement of other agencies in gathering and providing information, as appropriate;
- consultation with supervisor/manager;
- record of initial analysis;
- decisions on further action/no action;
- record of decisions/rationale with family/agencies;
- informing other agencies of the decisions;

- statement to the family of decisions made and, if a child is in need, the plan for providing support.

As part of any initial assessment, the child should be seen. This includes observation and talking with the child in an age appropriate manner. This is further discussed in paragraphs 3.41 to 3.43.

3.11   **A core assessment** is defined as an in-depth assessment which addresses the central or most important aspects of the needs of a child and the capacity of his or her parents or caregivers to respond appropriately to these needs within the wider family and community context. While this assessment is led by social services, it will invariably involve other agencies or independent professionals, who will either provide information they hold about the child or parents, contribute specialist knowledge or advice to social services or undertake specialist assessments. Specific assessments of the child and/or family members may have already been undertaken prior to referral to the social services department. The findings from these should inform this assessment. At the conclusion of this phase of assessment, there should be an analysis of the findings which will provide an understanding of the child's circumstances and inform planning, case objectives and the nature of service provision. The timescale for completion of the core assessment is a **maximum of 35 working days**. A core assessment is deemed to have commenced at the point the initial assessment ended, or a strategy discussion decided to initiate enquiries under s47, or new information obtained on an open case indicates a core assessment should be undertaken. Where specialist assessments have been commissioned by social services from other agencies or independent professionals, it is recognised that they will not necessarily be completed within the 35 working day period. Appropriate services should be provided whilst awaiting the completion of the specialist assessment.

3.12   The Department of Health has published an **Initial Assessment Record**, which has been developed for all staff to record salient information about a child's needs, the parents' capacity and the family's circumstances, to assist in determining the social services' response and whether a core assessment should be considered. This record is consistent with the **Core Assessment Record**. These have been developed to assist in assessing the child's developmental needs in an age appropriate manner for the following age bands: 0–2 years, 3–4 years, 5–9 years, 10–14 years and 15 and upwards. These age bands are the same as those used in **Looking After Children Assessment and Action Records** (Department of Health, 1995b). The initial and core assessment recording forms have been designed to assist in the analysis of a child and family's circumstances (Department of Health and Cleaver, 2000) and in the development and reviewing of a plan of action.

3.13   At the conclusion of either an initial or core assessment, the parent(s) and child, if appropriate, should be informed in writing, and/or in another more appropriate medium, of the decisions made and be offered the opportunity to record their views, disagreements and to ask for corrections to recorded information. Agencies and individuals involved in the assessment should also be informed of the decisions, with reasons for these made clear. This sharing of information is important to assist agencies' own practice in their work with the child and family. Local authorities are required by section 26 of the Children Act 1989 to establish complaints procedures, and children and parents should be provided with information about these. Parents

Figure 4 **Maximum Timescales for Analysing the Needs of Child and Parenting Capacity**

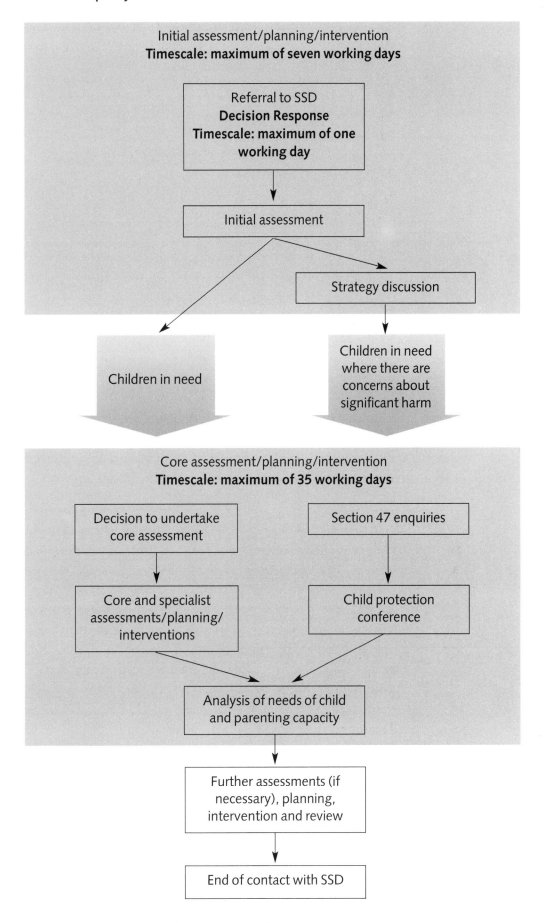

who have a complaint about a particular agency's services should take it up with the agency concerned.

3.14 The **maximum timescales** for completing an analysis of the needs of children and the parenting capacity to respond to those needs are represented in Figure 4. The needs of some children, in particular those who require emergency intervention, may mean that the initial assessment stage is brief. It may also be brief where the needs of the child can be determined in a period of less than seven working days. The same considerations apply to the minimum and maximum timescales for the core assessment.

S47 and Core Assessment

3.15 At any stage, should there be suspicions or allegations about child maltreatment and concern that the child may be or is likely to suffer significant harm, there must be strategy discussions and inter-agency action in accordance with the guidance in *Working Together to Safeguard Children* (1999). Assessment of what is happening to a child in these circumstances is not a separate or different activity but continues the same process, although the pace and scope of assessment may well have changed (see paragraphs 5.33 to 5.38 in *Working Together to Safeguard Children* (1999)). A key part of the assessment will be to establish whether there is reasonable cause to suspect that this child is suffering or is likely to suffer significant harm and whether any emergency action is required to secure the safety of the child.

3.15 The way in which the initial and core assessments have been integrated into the processes for children who are considered to be, or likely to be suffering significant harm are set out in Figure 5. This flow chart concerning individual cases is reproduced from *Working Together to Safeguard Children* (1999, p.116).

3.16 As indicated in paragraphs 5.39 to 5.41 of *Working Together to Safeguard Children* (1999) sometimes it will be appropriate to undertake an investigative interview of a child who may have been a victim to a crime or a witness, with a view to gathering evidence for criminal proceedings. These interviews should take account of information known from any previous assessments. A child should never be interviewed in the presence of an alleged or suspected perpetrator of abuse, or somebody who may be colluding with a perpetrator. The guidance (which is currently being revised) in the *Memorandum of Good Practice on video recorded interviews for child witnesses for criminal proceedings* (Home Office and Department of Health, 1992) should be followed for all video-recorded investigative interviews with children.

3.17 All such interviews with children should be conducted by those with specialist training and experience in interviewing children. Additional specialist help may be necessary if the child's first language is not English; the child appears to have a degree of psychiatric disturbance but is deemed competent; the child has an impairment; or where interviewers do not have adequate knowledge and understanding of the child's racial, religious or cultural background. Consideration should also be given to the gender of interviewers particularly in cases of alleged sexual abuse.

3.18 Following the publication of *Speaking Up For Justice* (Home Office, 1998), the report of the Working Group on Vulnerable or Intimidated Witnesses, Part II of the Youth

Figure 5 **Working Together to Safeguard Children
(Individual Cases Flowchart)**

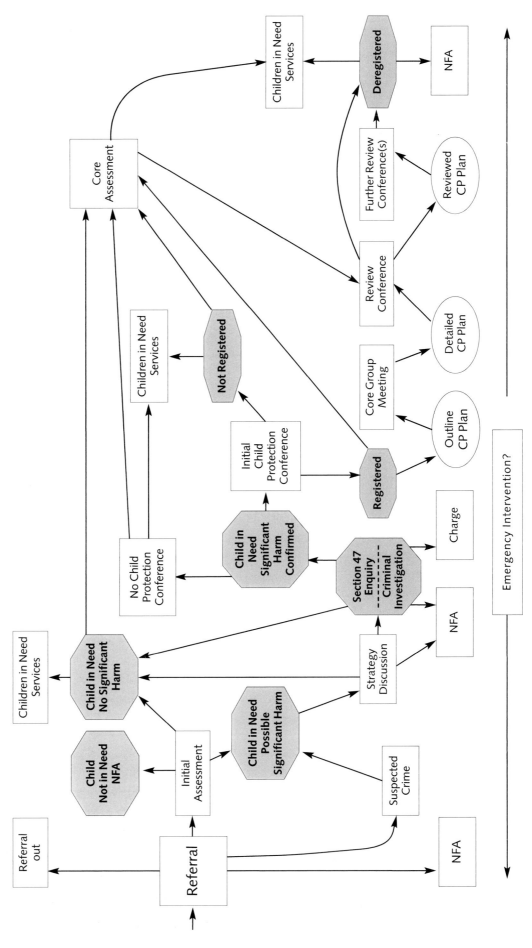

Justice and Criminal Evidence Act 1999 extends the range of measures available to assist child witnesses.

The Act provides different levels of protection for three groups of child witnesses according to the nature of assistance each group is considered to need. These are:

- All children in need of special protection – because they are giving evidence in a case that involves a sexual and/or violent offence – will give video-recorded evidence-in-chief unless this would not be in the interests of justice.

- Children under 17 who are giving evidence in a case involving violence, neglect, abduction or false imprisonment will be cross-examined via a live link at the trial.

- When facilities are available, children under 17 who are giving evidence in a sexual offence case will be cross-examined at a video-recorded pre-trial hearing unless the child informs the court that he would prefer to be cross-examined at trial (on live link or in court).

There is a presumption that all children who are giving evidence in cases involving other offences will give evidence-in-chief by means of a video recording, and will be cross-examined on live link at the trial.

3.19   The Act also provides a range of other measures to assist child witnesses including:

- assistance with communication;

- the use of an intermediary to assist with the questioning;

- screening the witness from the accused in court;

- the removal by judges of their wigs and gowns;

- clearing the public gallery in sexual offence cases.

The majority of these measures will be available to the Crown Court and youth courts by the end of 2000.

Use of Assessments in Family Proceedings

3.20   It may be appropriate to use evidence gathered during the assessment process for family proceedings. This may arise where an assessment has been completed **before** the commencing of proceedings or because it is necessary to undertake an assessment **during** the proceedings. The following paragraphs set out some issues around the interface between the assessment processes and reporting in writing in family proceedings.

3.21   The term **family proceedings** is one that is defined statutorily in section 8 of the Children Act 1989. It includes all public law applications (care, adoption, emergency protection, contact) and a large range of private law matters concerning divorce and separation, including those within applications under section 8 for contact, residence, specific issue and prohibited steps.

Care Applications and Assessment

3.22   In court proceedings involving the local authority, such as an application for a care or supervision order, the local authority's main evidence will be set out by way of one or more formal statements. These include the relevant history and the facts to support the **threshold criteria** (ie. significant harm) for an order under section 31. Information concerning the **welfare checklist** (section 1(3)) to which the court must have regard will also be included in the application.

3.23 Before making any order, the court must also consider the **no order principle** (section 1(5)). The court will look to the detail of the local authority's care plan for evidence as to how the care order, if made, would be implemented. Guidance about the structure and contents of care plans was issued in 1999 (*Care Plans and Care Proceedings under the Children Act 1989* LAC (99(29)).

3.24 Evidence arising from assessments may be used within the proceedings in one or more of the following ways by providing evidence:

- in support of the threshold criteria;

- around issues in the welfare checklist;

- about the rationale for the overall aim of the care plan or specific details within it (such as contact arrangements).

Disclosure

3.25 In family proceedings, documents produced by parties are normally shared among all parties – typically, the local authority, the parents and the guardian ad litem. It should be remembered that an assessment undertaken for the purpose of the proceedings will generate information for the **court** and this cannot, save exceptionally with the court's agreement, be withheld in full or in part because aspects may be unfavourable to one of the parties.

3.26 Assessments may be commissioned before the commencement of court proceedings or where such proceedings have not been anticipated. Where such an assessment includes information, opinions and recommendations from professionals not employed by the local authority (such as specialists in child and adolescent mental health), those persons should be advised that their contribution may be used in family proceedings.

3.27 Appendix D sets out a number of practice issues to be considered when using information gathered during assessment for family proceedings.

Court Sanctioned Assessments

3.28 A range of assessments may be made without legal restriction in respect of a child who is **not** the subject of care or related court applications.

3.29 Section 38(6) provides that where the Court makes an interim care order or interim supervision order it may give such directions (if any) as it considers appropriate with regard to the medical or psychiatric examination or other assessment of the child. By subsection (7) a direction may be to the effect that there is to be **no** such examination or assessment **unless** the Court directs otherwise.

3.30 Rule 18 of the Family Proceedings Courts (Children Act 1989) Rules 1991 provides that no person may without leave of the Justice's Clerk or the Court cause the child to be medically or psychiatrically examined, or otherwise assessed, for the purpose of the preparation of expert evidence for use in the proceedings. (See also paragraphs 3.61 to 3.62 in *An Introduction to the Children Act 1989* (1989) which deal with assessments in the context of care proceedings.) There are corresponding Rules for the County and High Court. Where care proceedings are underway, the nature and scope of any specialist assessment to be commissioned should be discussed in advance with legal advisers. Legal advisers will also help ensure that the implications of relevant case law, Practice Directions, Human Rights Act 1998, European Court of Human Rights judgments and other authoritative guidance are brought to the attention of those preparing assessments and subsequent reports for courts.

Oral Evidence

3.31 The assessment provides the basis for formal written evidence for use in the proceedings. However, it may be necessary for the professional(s) undertaking the assessment to give additional evidence orally. In family proceedings, there is less emphasis on restrictions such as hearsay and generally the proceedings are considered to be less adversarial than non-family cases. The key worker should liaise closely with the local authority legal department in anticipating those issues likely to be raised.

Working with Children and Families

3.32 Gathering information and making sense of a family's situation are key phases in the process of assessment. It is not possible to do this without the knowledge and involvement of the family. It requires direct work with children and with family members, explaining what is happening, why an assessment is being undertaken, what will be the process and what is likely to be the outcome. Gaining the family's co-operation and commitment to the work is crucially important. Families often have a number of fears and anxieties about approaching social services departments for help or about being referred to them by other agencies. Parents are fearful, for instance, that they will be perceived as failing in some way (Cleaver and Freeman, 1995; Aldgate and Bradley, 1999). They are also very clear about what they value from the professionals they meet, even in the most difficult circumstances. In particular, parents ask for clear explanations, openness and honesty, and to be treated with respect and dignity. Children's needs for explanations of what is happening may sometimes be overlooked. They should be informed clearly and sensitively even when they do not communicate through speech and where professionals may be unclear how much of what is being said is understood. They do not want to be kept in the dark or patronised. Studies have found that 'children are particularly sensitive to professionals who treat them personally, with care, and above all respect' (Jones and Ramchandani, 1999). It is especially important to help children handle uncertainty while plans are being formulated.

3.33 Different ways of providing explanations to families have been developed, some in written form accompanying the use of local authority records or materials for gathering information, which are shared with family members. An example of one such approach developed by a local authority is included above (Figure 6). Other local authorities have produced leaflets for families or use materials published by specialist

Figure 6 **Explaining Assessment to Family Members: An Example Accompanying a Written Record**

What is an assessment?

- Either you, or someone else on your behalf, has asked the social services departments for help with some difficulty you are having which affects your child (or children).

- Before we can help you, we need to know more about you and your family. This will involve collecting information, talking this through with you and agreeing what might be done. We call this an assessment.

Why is an assessment being carried out?

- Through making an assessment of your situation, it should be possible to see what help and support you and your family might need, and who could best give that help.

- Information will be gathered and written down. Although social workers and other professionals will normally take the lead in completing the assessment, this should always be done in a way which helps you to have your say, and encourages you to take part.

- Any information you give to us will be held in confidence within the social services department. If there is a need to discuss this information with anyone else, we will normally ask for your permission. The only exception to this is if information comes to light which, in the social worker's view, may indicate a serious threat to the welfare of your child. If this is the case, you will be told what your rights are in this new situation.

What will happen?

- Completing an assessment usually means the social worker will meet with you and members of your family a number of times.

- When children are old enough to take part in the assessment, the social worker will encourage and help them to do so.

- The assessment will take into consideration your ethnic and cultural background. If required, help will be provided in your first language.

- When other people are already helping you and your family, it is likely the social worker will talk to them too. We shall discuss this with you.

- If you do not agree with what the social worker says in the assessment, there will be an opportunity for you to record your point of view on the assessment record.

- The purpose of assessment is to draw up a plan of action to address the needs of your child (or children) and how you might need help to respond to these. You will be given a copy of the plan.

What will be expected of you?

- We know that almost all parents want to do their best for their children, and completing the assessment will help the social workers recognise the strengths you and your family have, as well as your difficulties.

- We can help you best if you tell us about what you do well in your family and your difficulties. We will keep you informed about what we are doing and thinking.

- An assessment is an important part of our working with you. In a very small number of cases, there are serious concerns about a child's safety. Making sure the child is safe will be our first concern. Please ask your social worker to explain this to you. You have a right to know.

What can you expect of us?

- We will listen carefully to what you have to say, offer advice and, if necessary, support to help you bring up your children and resolve your difficulties.

- We know that with a little help most families can sort out their own problems, and our aim is to help you do that.

- We will try our best to offer you any services you need as soon as possible. But there are often many more people needing services than there are services to give. This means that sometimes although everyone is agreed that you need a service, it might not be available at the time. If this happens we will always look to find an alternative, but we cannot guarantee to provide a particular service.

groups such as Family Rights Group, NSPCC or Who Cares? Trust. Key to the use of written materials is that they must be accompanied by direct communication and involvement by practitioners with family members and that repeated explanations may be necessary.

3.34 The issues of working with children and families where there are concerns that a child is being maltreated are explored in *The Challenge of Partnership in Child Protection* (Department of Health, 1995a). That publication provides detailed practice guidance about how to work with families throughout the process of enquiries being made and action taken to protect a child. It warns that 'those under the stress associated with allegations of child abuse may drift away from a working method which is sensitive to families' needs and which encourages their participation in the process' (p.46).

3.35 There will be situations where family members do not wish to work co-operatively with statutory agencies. This may be for a variety of reasons; they are too afraid or they believe they or their child have no problem or they are generally hostile to public welfare agencies. They may be resistant because of the nature of their own difficulties, such as psychiatric illness or problems of alcohol and drug misuse, or because of allegations being made against them. Whatever the reasons for their resistance, the door to co-operation should be kept open. At the very least, family members should be informed of what is happening and how they could participate more fully. Ways should be explored to engage some family members in the assessment process. The experience of research and practice confirms that, even after initial difficulties, the prospect of working in partnership with one or more family members may not be lost for ever, and that to do so will have long term beneficial outcomes for the child and family. The desirability of working with family members, however, must not override the importance of ensuring that children are safe.

3.36 Where there is resistance, 'a determination not to be overwhelmed, distracted or immobilised by the parents' initial response is essential' (Department of Health, 1995a). However, in a small number of instances, resistance to co-operation by a parent is accompanied by overtly aggressive, abusive or threatening behaviour or by more subtle underlying menace. Staff may be aware of the threat and in response either avoid family contact or unwisely place themselves in situations of danger (Cleaver *et al*, 1998). It is in these circumstances that access to available, skilled, expert supervision is essential so that the nature of the threat can be understood, the implications for the child and other family members identified and strategies found for maintaining work with the family. These may include co-working with experienced staff within or across agencies, changing times and venue for meetings with the family and other measures. Concerns about such matters should always be taken seriously and acted upon. It may be necessary to involve the expertise of professionals from a number of agencies to arrive at an understanding of the risks a particular individual may pose to the safety of staff, as well as to family members.

Planning Assessment

3.37 Gathering information requires careful planning. However difficult the circumstances, the **purpose** of assessing the particular child and the family should always be kept in mind and the impact of the process on the child and family considered. It has to be remembered that:

- the aim is to clarify and identity the needs of the child;

- the process of assessment should be helpful and as unintrusive to the child and family as possible;

- families do not want to be subjected to repeated assessments by different agencies;

- if, during the assessment, the child's safety is or becomes a concern, it must be secured before proceeding with the assessment.

3.38 It is essential, therefore, that the process of assessment should be carefully planned, whatever the pressure to begin work. 'Preparation, process and outcome are inextricably linked' (Adcock, 2000). This planning should take place in discussion with the child and family members unless to do so would place the child at increased risk of significant harm (*Working Together to Safeguard Children*, 1999, paragraph 5.6). As part of the preparation, key questions should be considered:

- Who will undertake the assessment and what resources will be needed?

- Who in the family will be included and how will they be involved (remembering absent or live-out family members, wider family and others significant to the child)?

- In what groupings will the child and family members be seen and in what order?

- Are there communication issues? If so, what are the specific communication needs and how will they be met?

- What methods of collecting information will be used? Which questionnaires and scales will be used?

- What information is already available?

- What other sources of knowledge about the child and family are available and how will other agencies and professionals who know the family be informed and involved? How will family members consent be gained?

- Where will assessment take place?

- What will be the timescale?

- How will information be recorded?

- How will it be analysed and who will be involved?

3.39   The nature of concerns about a child's needs will determine how the process is carried out and the extent of detail collected. The greater the concern, the greater the need for specificity, for use of specialist knowledge and judgement in the process and, therefore, the need for careful co-ordination and management of work with the family and other agencies. The more complex or difficult the child's situation, the more important it will be that multiple sources of information are used. These may include:

- **Direct work with the child** through shared activities, interviews, questionnaires, scales and play, which are age and culturally appropriate to the child's age, development and culture.

- **Direct work with the parents** through interviews with one or more parental members; parental discussions; taking parental histories; using scales, question-naires and other resources to gain a shared view of parental issues and parental functioning.

- **Direct work with the family** through interviews with the family in appropriate groupings of family members; taking family histories; using scales, questionnaires and other resources to gain a shared view of family issues and family functioning.

- **Direct work with the child and current caregivers**, if the child is not living with parents.

- **Observation** of the child alone and of the child/parent(s)/caregiver(s) interaction. Consideration should be given to doing this in the home, in school (both classroom and play areas) and with friends as well as family members.

- **Other sources of knowledge**, including those who have known the child over time, such as the midwife, health visitor, general practitioner, nursery staff or school teachers, and others who know the family such as staff from voluntary agencies, housing departments and adult health and social services. Other professionals may have become involved with the child or other children in the family for a specific purpose, for example educational psychologists, speech therapists, youth offending team members. Police and probation may also be important sources of information where there are concerns about a child or family members' safety.

- **Other information held on files and records and from previous assessments.** These should always be carefully checked as far as possible.

- **Specialist assessments** from a range of professionals may be commissioned to provide specific understanding about an aspect of the child's development, parental strengths and difficulties or the family's functioning. The timing of these and their particular contribution to the analysis of the child's needs and the plan of intervention will require careful consideration.

3.40   As a general principle, any records of assessments, plans or reports should be routinely shared with family members and children as appropriate, in addition to being shared with relevant professionals. These may require explanation and re-explanation to family members. Copies of assessments and plans, in their first language, should be given to family members wherever possible. Care should be taken to ensure that the meaning and implications of assessments are understood by the child and family members, as far as is possible.

Communicating with Children

3.41 In responding to a request for help or a referral, the importance of working with family members has been emphasised. However, if the process of assessment is to be child centred, an understanding of what is happening to the child cannot only be gained from information contributed by family members or other professionals who know the child. Direct work with children is an essential part of assessment, as well as recognising their rights to be involved and consulted about matters which affect their lives. This applies to all children, including disabled children. Communicating with some disabled children requires more preparation, sometimes more time and on occasions specialist expertise, and consultation with those closest to the child. For example, for children with communication difficulties it may be necessary to use alternatives to speech such as signs, symbols, facial expression, eye pointing, objects of reference or drawing. Communicating with a child with very complex difficulties may benefit from help of a third party who knows the child well and is familiar with the child's communication methods (see Chapter 3 in Department of Health, 2000a). Children whose first language is not English should have the opportunity to speak to a professional in their first language, wherever possible. It is particularly important at turning points in their lives that 'children are enabled to express their wishes and feelings; make sense of their circumstances and contribute to decisions that affect them' (NSPCC *et al*, 1997).

3.42 It is essential that a child's safety is addressed, if appropriate, during the course of undertaking direct work with him or her. There are five critical components in direct work with children: seeing, observing, talking, doing and engaging:

- **Seeing children**: an assessment cannot be made without seeing the child, however young and whatever the circumstances. The more complex or unclear a situation or the greater the level of concern, the more important it will be to see the child regularly and to take note of appearance, physical condition, emotional wellbeing, behaviour and any changes which are occurring.

- **Observing children**: the child's responses and interactions in different situations should be carefully observed wherever possible, alone, with siblings, with parents and/or caregivers or in school or other settings. Children may hide or suppress their feelings in situations which are difficult or unsafe for them, so it is important that general conclusions are not reached from only limited observations.

- **Engaging children**: this involves developing a relationship with children so that they can be enabled to express their thoughts, concerns and opinions as part of the process of helping them make real choices, in a way that is age and developmentally appropriate. Children should clearly understand the parameters within which they can exercise choice. In offering children such options, adults must not abdicate their responsibilities for taking decisions about a child's welfare.

- **Talking to children**: although this may seem an obvious part of communicating with children, it is clear from research that this is often not done at all or not done well. It requires time, skill, confidence and careful preparation by practitioners. Issues of geographical distance, culture, language or communication needs because of impairments may require specific consideration before deciding how best to communicate with the child. Children themselves are particularly sensitive to how and when professionals talk to them and consult them. Their views must be sought before key meetings. Again, a range of opportunities for talking to children may be needed, appropriate to the child's circumstances, age and stage of development, which may include talking to the child on their own, in a family meeting or accompanied by or with the assistance of a trusted person.

- **Activities with children**: undertaking activities with children can have a number of purposes and beneficial effects. It is important that they are activities which the child understands and enjoys, in which trust with the worker can develop and which give the child an experience of safety. They can allow positive interaction between the worker and the child to grow and enable the professional to gain a better understanding of the child's responses and needs.

3.43 Children have been asked what they consider to be good professional practice. They value social workers who:

> - **Listen** – carefully and without trivialising or being dismissive of the issues raised;
> - are **available and accessible** – regular and predictable contact;
> - are **non-judgemental and non-directive** – accepting, explaining and suggesting options and choices;
> - have a sense of **humour** – it helps to build a rapport;
> - are **straight-talking** – with realism and reliability; no 'false promises';
> - can be **trusted** – maintain **confidentiality** and consult with children before taking matters forward.
>
> Butler and Williamson (1994) reproduced from *Turning Points: A Resource Pack for Communicating with Children*. Introduction. pp. 1–2. (1997)

3.44 The exercise of professional judgement will be important in deciding when and how to communicate with children during the assessment process and how to interpret their communication in the context of the circumstances. Consideration should be given as to how children are informed and involved at each stage of the process, so that they have the opportunity to agree what the key issues are, what they would like to happen and to discuss what is possible and not possible. 'Children need to trust that they will be understood as individuals in their own right; usually they will want reassurance about what their parent/carer will be told about what they say' (Brandon, 1999).

3.45 Consideration of when and how to involve specific professionals with expertise and experience in assessing children's development will also be important throughout the assessment process. Professionals in a variety of child welfare agencies may be able to assist social services staff through discussion or advice based on their understanding and interpretation of information and views gathered from children. There may, however, be aspects of children's development and behaviour which require specialist assessment, either by joint work or referral to specific agencies. For example, assessing the strength of a child's attachment to a parent in circumstances of maltreatment or the educational potential of a school leaver who is living rough on the streets and seeking help. Children will require careful and straightforward explanations about why new professionals are being involved.

Consent and Confidentiality

3.46 When a family approaches social services for help or is referred, the family is generally the first and most important source of information about the child and the family's circumstances. However, in establishing whether this is a child in need and how best those needs may be met, it is likely to be important to gather information from a number of professionals who have contact with and knowledge of the child and family.

3.47 Personal information about children and families held by professionals and agencies is subject to a legal duty of confidence and should not normally be disclosed without the consent of the subject. However, the law permits the disclosure of confidential information if it is necessary to safeguard a child or children in the public interest: that is, the public interest in child protection may override the public interest in maintaining confidentiality. Disclosure should be justifiable in each case, according to the particular facts of the case, and legal advice should be sought in cases of doubt.

3.48 Children are entitled to the same duty of confidence as adults, provided that, in the case of those under 16 years of age, they have the ability to understand the choices and their consequences relating to any treatment. In exceptional circumstances, it may be believed that a child seeking advice, for example on sexual matters, is being exploited or abused. In such cases, confidentiality may be breached, following discussion with the child.

3.49 All agencies working with children and families should make their policies about sharing personal information available to users of their services and other agencies. This includes ensuring that such information is accessible and appropriate to children and families. Individual professionals should always make sure their agency's policies are known to the family with whom they are working. There will be variations in policy between agencies in accordance with their roles and responsibilities. Personal information about a child and family should always be respected but, in order to achieve good outcomes for the child, it may be appropriate to share it between professionals and teams within the same agency. Sensitive and careful judgements are required in the child's best interests.

3.50 In obtaining consent to seek information from other parties or to disclose information about the child or other individuals under the Data Protection Act 1998 it is important that explanations include:

- clarity about the purpose of approaching other individuals or agencies;

- reasons for disclosure of any information, for example about the referral or details about the child or family members;

- details of the individuals or agencies being contacted;

- what information will be sought or shared;

- why the information is important;

- what it is hoped to achieve.

3.51 The **Data Protection Act 1998** allows for disclosure without the consent of the subject in certain conditions, including for the purposes of the prevention or detection of crime, or the apprehension or prosecution of offenders, and where failure to disclose would be likely to prejudice those objectives in a particular case.

3.52 Article 8 of the **European Convention on Human Rights** states that:

(1) Everyone has the right to respect for his private and family life, his home and his correspondence.

(2) There shall be no interference by a public authority with the exercise of this right except such as in accordance with the law and is necessary in a democratic society in the interests of national security, public safety or the economic wellbeing of the country, for the prevention of disorder or crime, for the protection of health or morals, or for the protection of the rights and freedoms of others.

3.53 Disclosure of information without consent might give rise to an issue under Article 8. Disclosure of information to safeguard children will usually be for the protection of health or morals, for the protection of the rights and freedoms of others, and for the prevention of disorder or crime. Disclosure should be appropriate for the purpose and only to the extent necessary to achieve that purpose.

3.54 Obtaining consent and respecting confidentiality may not always be straightforward, particularly in situations of family conflict or dispute, or where a number of parental figures including absent parents are involved or where there are allegations of abuse about which enquiries are being made. The consent of any one parent acting alone, rather than all those with parental responsibility, is required to disclose information about a child (section 2(7) of the Children Act 1989).

3.55 Where there are concerns that a child may be suffering or is likely to suffer significant harm, it is essential that professionals and other people share information for it is often 'only when information from a number of sources has been shared and is then put together that it becomes clear that a child is at risk of or is suffering harm' (*Working Together to Safeguard Children*, 1999, paragraph 7.27). Unless to do so would place the child or children at increased risk of significant harm the nature of the child protection concerns should be explained to family members and to children, where appropriate, and their consent to contact other agencies sought. This requires careful explanation in plain language. It may be helpful to have written as well as verbal explanations (an example of this is the statement for family members on pages 39 and 40). For some families under stress or coping in difficult circumstances, explanations may need to be repeated several times. In all cases where the police are involved the decision about when to inform the parents will have a bearing on the conduct of police investigations and should inform part of the strategy discussion.

3.56 In any potential conflict between the responsibilities of professionals towards children and towards other family members, the needs of the child must come first. Where there are concerns that a child is or may be at risk of suffering significant harm, the overriding principle must be to safeguard the child. In such cases, when it is considered that a child may be in danger or that a crime is being or has been committed, the duty of confidence can be overridden. However, it will be important that the respective duties and powers of different agencies are clearly understood by all parties.

3.57 These matters are fully discussed in paragraphs 7.27 to 7.46 of *Working Together to*

Safeguard Children (1999) in the context of the legal framework and professional guidelines for different agencies. In this publication, Appendix E reproduces an abridged version of the Data Protection Registrar's checklist for setting up information sharing arrangements.

Assessment of Children in Special Circumstances

3.58 Some of the children referred for help because of the nature of their problems or circumstances, will require particular care and attention during assessment. These are children who may become lost to the statutory agencies, whose wellbeing or need for immediate services may be overlooked and for whom subsequent planning and intervention may be less than satisfactory. This may be for a number of reasons including the following:

- They are **children in transition**. For example, their families may be moving from one geographical location to another; they may be moving schools, leaving school or leaving care, or moving into young adulthood and into the remit of adult rather than children's services. They may be disabled young people and their families, moving from child to adult services (Morris, 1999). They may be part of a travelling community or in families based periodically overseas, such as the armed forces.

- They are **children in hospital** for long periods of time. Under section 85 of the Children Act 1989 the social services department has a duty to assess the welfare of a child in hospital for longer than three months consecutively. This assessment is to ascertain whether the child's welfare is being adequately safeguarded and promoted and whether the child and their family require services.

- They (or their parents) have specific **communication needs**, for example they do not use English as a first language, or they do not communicate through speech.

- They (or their families, including siblings) have **a long history of contact with social services** and other child welfare agencies. Their circumstances may be chaotic; files numerous; many staff may have been involved; they may not currently have an allocated worker. Any of these circumstances may result in the need for assessment or reassessment at this point in time not being recognised.

- They are children whose problems or those of their parents are **not sufficiently serious to receive services** under social services priorities. These children's health or development may not be considered to be being impaired, but an analysis of the risk factors and stressors in their lives would suggest they are likely to suffer impairment in the future. What is required is recognition of the interaction of child and/or parental problems on a child's health and development and the cumulative effect of such problems over time. For example, a mother with a mild learning disability may not reach the criteria for help from an adult services team and her child's standard of care may not be sufficiently poor to meet the criteria for children's services intervention. However, the failure to recognise the need for early intervention to provide support to the child and family on a planned basis from both children's and adult's services may result in the child's current and future development being impaired.

- They are **children and young people involved in the use of drugs** where the level and nature of their drug use is unknown to their parents and/or any professionals to whom they are known, for example, teachers, although their general health or behaviour may be a cause for concern. These children may be fearful of asking for help from statutory agencies and may be more receptive to approaches from voluntary agencies or specialist drug services.

- They are young people about whom there are concerns that they are becoming or might be **involved in prostitution**. Draft government *Guidance on Children Involved in Prostitution*, issued for consultation in December 1998, sets out an inter-agency approach to helping this group of young people. The emphasis is on both preventing these vulnerable children from becoming involved in prostitution and safeguarding and promoting the welfare of those who are being abused through prostitution. These situations may require careful assessment of the young person's needs and consideration of how best to help him or her.

- They are children **separated from their country of origin** who are without the care and protection of their parents or legal guardian, often referred to as **unaccompanied asylum seeking children**. Their status, age and circumstances may all be uncertain, in addition to their having experienced or witnessed traumatic events, and they may be suffering the most extreme forms of loss. The situations in which they are accommodated, albeit on a temporary basis, may be less than adequate, for example, where an 18 year old Eritrean young woman is caring for her 10 year old brother in bed and breakfast accommodation for homeless people. There is a helpful *Statement of Good Practice* (Separated Children in Europe Programme, 1999) which provides a straightforward account of the policies and practice required to act to protect the rights of such children.

- They are **children of asylum seeking families** who may have extensive unmet needs while the focus of activity is on resolving the adults' asylum applications, accommodation or other pressing issues.

- They have **a parent in prison**. It is estimated that 125,000 children have a parent in prison at any one time (Ramsden, 1998). In 1997, approximately 8,000 women were received into the prison system (either untried and/or following custodial sentences). A survey by the Home Office (Caddle and Crisp, 1997) suggests that over 60% have children under the age of 18 and over half the women have had their first or only child as teenagers. At the very least, children in these circumstances experience disruptions in their care, but for some the consequences are much more severe and long lasting. Furthermore, social services departments may be asked by the Prison Service to contribute to assessments when there are children involved (See paragraph 5.82).

3.59 There are common features which apply to the assessment of children in all these and other similar situations:

- they require a high degree of co-operation and co-ordination between staff in different agencies, in planning or preparing for assessments, in undertaking and completing them;

- extra care must be taken to ensure that there is an holistic view of the child and that the child does not become lost between the agencies involved and their different systems and procedures;

- as most children are registered with a GP, this route could be used for locating lost children and obtaining information about their past histories;

- particular attention should be given to health and education assessments of these children. The older the child, the more these may be overlooked or found difficult to arrange;

- consideration must be given to the means by which information will be analysed and action planned, how the outcome of assessment is communicated and to whom;

- responsibility for action and providing services must be clearly identified and recorded, with specific timescales;

- overall responsibility for ensuring the welfare of the child in need must be clearly allocated.

3.60 It is significant that, where adolescents are the subject of assessment, studies emphasise the importance of staff finding time to engage in direct work with young people and getting to know them well, although it may be difficult sometimes 'to get below the surface' (Sinclair *et al*, 1995). Sadly, such studies reveal that all too often assessments with older children fail to be completed, especially where specialist professional assessments are required. Even greater efforts are necessary to co-ordinate and achieve co-operation from all parties in these situations.

Assessing the Needs of Young Carers

3.61 A group of children whose needs are increasingly more clearly recognised are young carers for example those who assume important caring responsibilities for parents and siblings. Some children care for parents who are disabled, physically or mentally ill, others for parents dependent on alcohol or involved in drug misuse. For further information and guidance refer to the *Carers (Recognition and Services) Act 1995: Policy Guidance and Practice Guide* (Department of Health, 1996a) and *Young Carers: Making a Start* (Department of Health, 1998a).

3.62 An assessment of family circumstances is essential. Young carers should not be expected to carry inappropriate levels of caring which have an adverse impact on their development and life chances. It should not be assumed that children should take on similar levels of caring responsibilities as adults. Services should be provided to parents to enhance their ability to fulfil their parenting responsibilities. There may be differences of view between children and parents about appropriate levels of care. Such differences may be out in the open or concealed. The resolution of such tensions will require good quality joint work between adult and children's social services as well as co-operation from schools and health care workers. This work should include direct work with the young carer to understand his or her perspective and opinions. The young person who is a primary carer of his or her parent or sibling may have a good understanding of the family's functioning and needs which should be incorporated into the assessment.

3.63 Young carers can receive help from both local and health authorities. Where a child is providing a substantial amount of care on a regular basis for a parent, the child will be entitled to an assessment of their ability to care under section 1(1) of the *Carers (Recognition and Services) Act 1995* and the local authority must take that assessment into account in deciding what community care services to provide for the parent. Many young carers are not aware that they can ask for such an assessment. In addition, consideration must be given as to whether a young carer is a child in need under the Children Act 1989. The central issue is whether a child's welfare or development might suffer if support is not provided to the child or family. As part of the *National Strategy for Carers* (1999a), local authorities should take steps to identify children with additional family burdens. Services should be provided to promote the health and development of young carers while not undermining the parent.

The Assessment Framework and Children Looked After

3.64 The Assessment Framework has been designed to assess children's needs across the same developmental dimensions as the Looking After Children materials (Parker (eds), 1991; Department of Health, 1995b). This will enable the Looking After Children system to be revised during 1999–2001 in a way which will result in an integrated model for assessing and providing services to the wider group of children in need and their families than looked after children. Most children who come into contact with social services departments do not enter the care system. However, should a child need to be looked after, congruence in the system will ensure that good quality baseline information is available about the child's developmental and wider needs at the point of entry to the looked after system. This will support improved assessment of the child's needs which will enable better placement matching in foster and residential care. The parenting capacity domain within the Assessment Framework can also be used with foster carers in assessing suitability for a particular child. It will also inform the provision of services to children and birth and foster families during the care episode. When children return home, or are placed with a permanent substitute family, using the same Assessment Framework will ensure continuity of planning to secure the best outcomes for the child.

3.65 The parenting capacity dimensions in the Assessment Framework will be particularly useful for evaluating improvements in parenting capacities as part of any decision making processes and, where appropriate, a reunification programme. This information will also be important in planning and managing contact. Once baseline information on parenting capacity has been collected during the core assessment, it will be possible to identify key areas for change and target social work and other resources more effectively whilst the child is looked after and reunification plans are being implemented. It should also enable social workers to decide when family reunification will not be possible and an alternative placement is required.

Children Being Placed for Adoption

3.66 In circumstances where there are children for whom adoption is planned, the Assessment Framework may be used as part of the assessment of the capacities of potential adopters, matching children with approved adopters, and planning what kinds of services a child and adopting parents might benefit from post placement and post adoption. These services might include help to understand any specific needs the child has and how best to respond to them. Some needs may require time limited interventions whereas others may exist on a continuing basis. The medical adviser to the social services department has a critical role to play in offering advice and information from the point at which a child is being considered for adoption and throughout the adoption process. A holistic approach to the consideration of what are likely to be complex needs of the child requires good inter-disciplinary co-operation and co-ordination.

Children Leaving Care

3.67 Where children leave care and live independently of their families, family links often remain very important. Research has pointed to the considerable potential of working in partnership with the child and their family during this transition period (Marsh and Peel, 1999).

3.68 The Children (Leaving Care) Bill which has been introduced in the 1999/2000 Parliamentary Session will, subject to Royal Assent, provide for every looked after child to have a personal adviser and a pathway plan by their sixteenth birthday. The pathway plan will be informed by an assessment of need based on the Assessment Framework and will, in effect, extend existing assessment and planning requirements to cover the child's transition to adulthood. The plan will be subject to regular review irrespective of whether the child remains looked after or has left care and the Bill provides for the continuation of the plan and contact by the personal adviser until the young person reaches the age of 21 and, where supported in higher education and training, up to the age of 24.

4

Analysis, Judgement and Decision Making

Treatment itself is intimately bound up with assessment, relying on it as a house relies on its foundation. Consequently, assessment continues throughout the treatment process, despite a change in focus during its course (Jones, 1997).

4.1 The Guidance has emphasised that assessment is not an end in itself but a process which will lead to an improvement in the wellbeing or outcomes for a child or young person. The conclusion of an assessment should result in:

- an analysis of the needs of the child and the parenting capacity to respond appropriately to those needs within their family context;

- identification of whether and, if so, where intervention will be required to secure the wellbeing of the child or young person;

- a realistic plan of action (including services to be provided), detailing who has responsibility for action, a timetable and a process for review.

4.2 Generally, all these phases of the assessment process should be undertaken in partnership with the child and key family members, and with their agreement. This includes finalising the plan of action. There may be exceptions when there are concerns that a child is suffering or may be suffering significant harm.

4.3 In many approaches or referrals to social services departments, families are clear about their problems but may not be sure where to turn or how to obtain services. With advice and information, they are able to take appropriate action. This action may be all that is required by a social services department. Where there is a question about whether a child is in need and therefore services are necessary an assessment is required. For some families, the process of assessment is in itself a therapeutic intervention. Being able to look at problems in a constructive manner with a professional who is willing to listen and who helps family members to reflect on what is happening, is enough to help them find solutions. During the assessment process, it may emerge that families will best be helped by agencies other than social services. Armed with this information, families may wish to seek solutions themselves; others may wish to have help in gaining access to other agencies or practical services.

4.4 A significant proportion of families who seek help from social services are unable to resolve stresses or problems solely from within their own emotional or practical resources or from their own support network. It is for these families that assessment may be important in order to identify the nature of their children's needs and, simultaneously, may be the first stage in a longer process of positive intervention. Ultimately, careful judgements must be made about balancing the needs of children and parents.

4.5 In most situations, meeting children's needs will almost always involve responding also to the needs of family members. The two are closely connected and it is rarely possible to promote the welfare of children without promoting the welfare of significant adults in their lives. In some cases, meeting the children's needs may mean giving others either parenting responsibility or legal parental responsibility for the child, either for short periods or on a longer term basis. Where consideration is being given to meeting parents' needs, as part of the plan of intervention, this must be because it is in the best interests of the child and will assist in securing better outcomes for the child. Parents may also require help in their own right as adults who have specific needs.

Analysis

4.6 In Chapter 3 it was emphasised that gathering information is a crucial phase in the assessment process, which requires careful planning about how best to undertake it. Information may be gathered from a variety of sources, using methods which will be determined by the purpose of the assessment and the particular circumstances of each child and family (see paragraph 3.38). Some of the information may have been gathered through the use of questionnaires and scales, such as those published in the accompanying materials (Department of Health, Cox and Bentovim, 2000). The **Home Inventory** (Caldwell and Bradley, 1984) and the **Assessment of Family Competence, Strengths and Difficulties** (Bentovim and Bingley Miller, forthcoming), due for publication later in 2000 will also provide important information about the child's world and family functioning respectively.

4.7 The information should be organised according to the dimensions of the Assessment Framework as a necessary beginning to the next phase of analysis. Information should be summarised under each of the three domains ie. children's developmental needs, parents' or caregivers' capacities to respond, and wider family and environmental factors. The Department of Health has developed assessment recording forms to assist practitioners and their managers in this phase of work (Department of Health and Cleaver, 2000).

4.8 In organising the information, there may be different perspectives to be explored, recorded and taken into account, for example, the child may have a different understanding and interpretation of what is happening from that of either parent or of a professional. These differences are important when developing an understanding of the child's needs within the family context. Different family members may attach different meanings to the same information, for example, the significance of past family history or events. The same information may vary in its salience for different family members, for example, the impact of a bereavement in a family. Sometimes these differences in perception can lead to conflicts in the family or between family members and professionals. In reaching a shared understanding of what is happening in a family, it is important to keep the focus on the needs of the child. This enables family members and professionals to agree a plan of action, even in the context of some differences or tensions, that will address the identified needs of the child with the aim of improving outcomes for the child.

4.9 By this point, there should be clear summaries which identify from the information gathered the child's developmental needs, parenting capacity and family and environmental factors. In each of these domains, both strengths and difficulties should be identified. Children's needs do not exist in a vacuum (Jones, 2000) and, therefore, the inter-relationships between the child, family and environment must be understood. Some factors will work positively to support children's growing up while others will militate against or undermine their healthy development. In weighing up the impact that various factors have on a child, it has to be borne in mind that not all factors will have equal significance and the cumulative effect of some relatively minor factors may be considerable. Thus the analysis of a child's needs is a complex activity drawing on knowledge from research and practice combined with an understanding of the child's needs within his or her family.

4.10 The elements of parenting capacity can be described, and minimum parenting standards or requirements assessed by the practitioner and related to their child. However, it is not possible to ascribe numerical values to each element because parenting capabilities and behaviours are complex and subject to influences from within and outside the family (Jones, 2000). Parenting capacity can only be understood within the overall context in which children are being brought up. The analysis should identify the family and environmental factors which have an impact on the different aspects of the child's development and on the parent(s) capacity in order to explore the relationship between the three domains (Department of Health and Cleaver, 2000). At some points in time judgements may be made (based on the analysis of their parental functioning) that the parent is unable to respond to their child's needs.

4.11 To summarise the analysis stage:

- A child's needs must be based on knowledge of what would be expected of this child's development;

- Parenting capacity should draw on knowledge about what would be reasonable to expect of parental care given to a similar child;

- Family and environmental factors should draw on knowledge about the impact these will have on both parenting capacity and directly on a child's development.

Judgements

4.12 Professionals will be drawing on their respective knowledge bases to inform the judgements they come to about a child's circumstances, whether the child is in need and whether their health and development is likely to be impaired without the provision of services. For some children, decisions will also have been made about whether they are suffering or are likely to suffer significant harm. The knowledge base will include information about the factors which are intrinsic to all children such as temperament, genetic make-up and race, and other factors which may be intrinsic to some children, such as physical or sensory impairments.

4.13 Critical to an understanding of what is happening to a child is the knowledge of the way in which children need to achieve certain tasks at particular ages and stages of development. Bentovim (1998) summarises current views on child development which 'emphasise that what matters for development is that the various systems – biological and psychological – should be well integrated. Development is about progression, change and re-organisation throughout life' (p.66). This normal pattern of development may not be achieved for some children either because of unavoidable factors such as impairments or because they are suffering significant harm (Bentovim, 1998).

4.14 There is a considerable literature to assist professionals when making a judgement about a parent's capacity and assessing what is a reasonable standard of care (Jones, 2000; Cleaver *et al*, 1999) 'even though research cannot provide the kind of numerical accuracy which is often sought' (Jones, 2000).

4.15 Critical at this phase will be judgements about a number of key issues (Jones, 1998):

- determining what has been happening and whether this is a child in need or is suffering significant harm;

- understanding the child and family context sufficiently to be able to secure the child's wellbeing or safety;

- assessing the likelihood of change;

  and later

- reviewing whether such change is being achieved.

4.16 It is important to identify strengths in the child's family system and to use these areas as the basis on which the child's development can be promoted. The more complex the family's problems, the more these will involve sophisticated inter-disciplinary and inter-agency co-operation in order to reach judgements about these issues. Stevenson (1998) provides a cautionary note in such circumstances. 'The families themselves may seem overwhelmed to the point of powerlessness, so the workers may experience similar feelings' (p.18). The reflective process for professionals working with children and families may be stressful, particularly in difficult circumstances. Some children's lives are such that profound, sensitive judgements may be required. This could include judgements about medical treatment in life threatening situations; judgements about whether to separate a child from his or her parents or caregivers; judgements about whether to place children with permanent substitute families. However, careful and systematic gathering of information, and its summary and analysis according to the framework can assist professionals in making sound evidence based judgements. The practice guidance has been developed to assist this process (Department of Health, 2000a).

4.17 Sometimes, where there are multi-faceted problems, assessments can become stuck and little progress made. Reder and Duncan (1999) talk about the danger of **assessment paralysis** which they describe as 'an impasse in the professional network where the issue of whether the parent has a psychiatric diagnosis becomes the context for deciding about all interventions'. Assessment paralysis can apply in other situations, where the focus of attention becomes stuck on a particular diagnostic issue and decision making is driven by this consideration rather than the child's needs. It requires vigilance and careful management by those staff who hold responsibility for the child's welfare to ensure that progress continues to be made to help the child.

Use of Consultation

4.18 Social services departments have lead responsibility for undertaking assessments of children in need. In order to arrive at well balanced judgements about the needs of children, practitioners and their managers may benefit from the expertise and experience of professionals in other disciplines. These professionals can act as consultants or advisers to assist and contribute to the assessment processes, which includes analysis of information gathered. This type of input may be as useful to the assessment as the commissioning of specialist assessments.

4.19 In some situations, where the available evidence requires careful analysis by those with particular expertise, sufficient information about a child and the family may already be available. Therefore, the specialist task is to assist in the analysis of available material, drawing on knowledge in particular areas about likely outcomes of certain courses of action. This expert knowledge can assist the practitioner and his or her manager when constructing a plan and deciding how to implement it.

Decision Making

4.20 In drawing up a plan of intervention, careful distinction should to be made between **judgements** about the child's developmental needs and parenting capacity and **decisions** about how best to address these at different points in time. These decisions will have to take account of a number of factors including:

- how existing good relationships and experiences can be nurtured and enhanced;

- what type of interventions are known to have the best outcomes for the particular circumstances of the child who has been assessed as in need;

- what the child and family can cope with at each stage. Complicated arrangements regarding the provision of services and interventions might well overwhelm the child or individual family members;

- how the necessary resources can be mobilised within the family's network and within professional agencies, including social services;

- what alternative interventions are available if the resources of choice cannot be secured;

- ensuring interventions achieve early success and have a beneficial impact. The self-esteem of children and parents is critical to the outcome of longer term intervention. Good experiences are important when many other aspects of family life may be in chaos or problems feel insurmountable;

- there may be an optimal hierarchy of interventions which will require distinguishing between what is achievable in the short term, what will have maximum impact on the child and family's wellbeing and what are the long term goals;

- identifying what the child regards as highest priority, for example, learning to ride a bicycle may be far higher on a child's list of wants than therapy, and such practical wishes should be taken account of because they may result in changes which will enable the child to make use of therapeutic help.

- It will be essential to achieve some parts of a proposed intervention within a predetermined timescale, in order to meet the child's needs. Other components of a plan will be less pressing and although desirable to achieve, not considered necessary for the prevention of future significant harm.

4.21 Underlying these critical considerations is the importance of keeping the child at the centre of the planning processes. Three key aspects of a child's health and development must inform the content and timing of the plan:

- ensuring the child's safety;

- remembering that a child cannot wait indefinitely;

- maintaining a child's learning.

4.22 The development of secure parent-child attachments is critical to a child's healthy development. The quality and nature of the attachment will be a key issue to be considered in decision making, especially if decisions are being made about moving a child from one setting to another, or re-uniting a child with his or her birth family. (For further discussion of attachment see Crittenden and Ainsworth, 1989; Schofield, 1998; Howe, 2000).

4.23 In complex situations, it may be helpful for those involved in the assessment process to meet to discuss the findings and formulate the plan. This should involve the parents and, as appropriate, the child. Family Group Conferences or multi-disciplinary meetings may provide for the construction of plans for children in need. *Working Together to Safeguard Children* (1999) sets out the processes to be followed for children about whom there are concerns that they are suffering or likely to suffer significant harm. The role of the key worker appointed when a child's name has been placed on a child protection register, the role of the group of professionals responsible for developing and implementing the child protection plan and the aims, content and processes for constructing such a plan are set out in paragraphs 5.75 to 5.84 of *Working Together to Safeguard Children* (1999).

4.24 For some families, the findings from the core assessment will indicate that the parents are responding appropriately to their child's needs, but in order to maximise the child's health and developmental outcomes, specific services are required to assist the parents and/or the child. In the absence of particular stress factors, such as those resulting from having a chronically ill child, the parents would be able to bring up their children without external help. However, the presence of these stressors require parents and families to develop new ways of functioning, as well as to accept support from outside their family and friendship networks. In these families, siblings may be affected significantly and services should address their needs.

4.25 It has to be recognised that in families where a child has been maltreated there are some parents who will not be able to change sufficiently within the child's timescales in order to ensure their children do not continue to suffer significant harm (Jones, 1998). In these situations, decisions may need to be made to separate permanently the child and parent or parents. In these circumstances decisions about the nature and form of any contact will also need to be made, in the light of all that is known about the child and the family, and reviewed throughout childhood. Key in these considerations is what is in the child's best interests, informed by the child's views (Cleaver, 2000).

4.26 The following criteria have been identified as suggesting a poor outcome for reuniting children who have been maltreated with their parents (Bentovim *et al*, 1987; Silvester *et al*, 1995):

- the abusing parent completely or significantly denies any responsibility for the child's developmental state or abuse;

- the child is rejected or blamed outright;

- the child's needs are not recognised by their parents who put their own needs first;

- parents have frequently failed to show concern, or acknowledge, long-standing difficulties such as alcoholism or psychiatric problems;

- during therapeutic interventions, the relationships within the family and with professionals remain at breaking point.

4.27 However, most parents are capable of change, and following appropriate interventions, able to provide a safe family context for their child. At times, children may need to be separated temporarily from their parent or parents. This enables change to take place while the child is living away from home in a safe environment. During this time, it will be important to address the changes required in the parent(s) as well as meeting any therapeutic needs of the child and other family members by active programmes of intervention, appropriate deployment of resources and careful review of progress. If a child is separated from their parent(s), it is essential that parents are able to sustain any improvements made whilst the child is living away from home, when the child returns to live with them. Careful thought should be given to the nature of services required by the parents and child during this transition phase, to ensure that earlier achievements are able to be maintained and continue to be improved upon. For some families continued intervention may be necessary for a considerable length of time until the child is no longer vulnerable.

4.28 Jones (1998, p.108) summarising relevant child maltreatment research findings reports the following features as having been identified in those cases where there are better prospects of achieving good outcomes for children:

- Those infants and children who despite abuse do not have residual disability, developmental delay or special educational needs;

- Those children subjected to less severe abuse or neglect;

- Children who have had the benefit of non-abusive or corrective relationships with peers, siblings and/or a supportive adult;

- Children who have developed more healthy and appropriate attributions about the maltreatment which they had suffered;

- Children and families who are able and willing to co-operate with helping agencies;

- Children and families who have been able to engage in therapeutic work;

- Situations where successful partnerships between professionals and family members have occurred;

- Children and families where the psychological abuse component of the maltreatment experience has been amenable to change.

4.29 When an analysis of a child's needs and parenting capacity within their family context is completed, there is then a baseline from which further assessment and re-assessment, using the Assessment Framework, can be undertaken to review progress as services are provided.

4.30 In a number of family situations where there is concern about a child's safety and future wellbeing whilst living in his or her family, the findings from a core assessment may provide an uncertain picture of the family's capacity to change. These families are characterised by one or more of the following (Bentovim *et al*, 1987; Silvester *et al*, 1995):

- uncertainty as to whether the parents are taking full responsibility for either the abuse or the child's developmental state;

- whereas the child's needs may sometimes be viewed as primary, the parents put their own needs as dominant;

- the child may be scape-goated and parent-child attachments are ambivalent or anxious;

- family patterns are rigid rather than healthily flexible;

- relationships with professionals are ambivalent.

4.31 These families often cause professionals considerable concern. It is important that services are provided to give the family the best chance of achieving the required changes. It is equally important that in circumstances where the family situation is not improving or changing fast enough to respond to the child's needs, decisions are made about the longterm future of the child. Delay or drift can result in the child not receiving the help she or he requires and having their health and development impaired.

Plans for Children in Need

4.32 The details of the plan are bench marks against which the progress of the family and the commitment of workers are measured, and therefore it is important that they should be realistic and not vague statements of good intent (Department of Health, 1995).

4.33 The analysis, judgement and decisions made will form the basis of a plan of work with a child in need and his or her family. The complexity or severity of the child's needs will determine the scope and detail of the plan. The different circumstances under which the assessment has been carried out will also determine the form in which it is recorded and the status of the plan:

- **Children in Need Plan** at the conclusion of a core assessment, which will involve the child and family members as appropriate and the contributions of all agencies.

A format for the plan is contained in assessment records (Department of Health and Cleaver, 2000).

- **Child Protection Plan** as a decision of an inter-agency child protection conference, following enquiries and assessment under s47. The expectations of a child protection plan are outlined in paragraphs 5.81 to 5.84 of *Working Together to Safeguard Children* (1999).

- **Care Plan for a Child Looked After** as a result of an assessment that a child will need to be looked after by the local authority either in the short term or long term and placed in foster or residential care. The requirements for a care plan in these circumstances are laid out in Volume 3 of the Children Act 1989, Guidance and Regulations (paragraphs 2.59 to 2.62). A format for the care plan is an integral part of the Department of Health's Looking After Children materials (Department of Health, 1995b).

- **Care Plans** for a child who is the subject of a care or supervision order or for whom the plan is adoption (see paragraphs 3.22 to 3.24).

- **Pathway Plan for a young person who is in care or leaving care** as outlined in the Government's intentions for young people living in and leaving care (Department of Health, 1999f; Children (Leaving Care) Bill, 1999).

4.34 There are some general principles about plans for working with children and families, whatever the circumstances in which they have been drawn up. First that, wherever possible, they should be drawn up in agreement with the child/young person and key family members and their commitment to the plan should have been secured. There are two caveats which the professionals responsible for the plan need to bear in mind:

- objectives should be reasonable and timescales not too short or unachievable;

- plans should not be dependent on resources which are known to be scarce or unavailable.

Failure to address these issues can be damaging to families and jeopardise the overall aim of securing the child's wellbeing. Second, the plan must maintain a focus on the child, even though help may be provided to a number of family members as part of the plan. As Jones *et al* (1987) write 'It is never acceptable to sacrifice the interests of the child for the therapeutic benefit of the parents'.

4.35 Department of Health practice guidance (1995a) recommended that professional workers and relevant family members should be clear about the following aspects of the plan which have general application (an abridged list is in Figure 7). With clarity about these matters, it is possible for both professionals and the family to take issue with the other when their expectations are not met or when perceptions and objectives begin to differ.

4.36 Fundamental to the plan, from the beginning, is the commitment of all the parties involved and the signatures to the plan of those who have lead responsibility for ensuring it is carried forward (in social services, this should include the team manager/supervisor as well as the practitioners). There should also be a clear recorded statement on the plan about when and how it will be reviewed. Reviewing the child's progress and the effectiveness of services and other interventions is a continuous part

Figure 7 AREAS IN WHICH CLARITY IS REQUIRED IN CHILD CARE PLANNING

- the objective of the plan, for example to provide and evaluate the efficacy of therapeutic interventions
- what services will be provided by which professional group or designated agency
- the timing and nature of contact between the professional workers and the family
- the purpose of services and professional contact
- specific commitments to be met by the family, for example attendance at a family centre
- specific commitments to be met by the professional workers, for example the provision of culturally sensitive services or special assistance for those with disabilities
- which components of the plan are negotiable in the light of experience and which are not
- what needs to change and the goals to be achieved, for example the child's weight to increase by a specific amount in a particular period, regular and appropriate stimulation for the child in keeping with her or his development and age
- what is unacceptable care of the child
- what sanctions will be used if the child is placed in danger or in renewed danger
- what preparation and support the child and adults will receive if she or he appears in court as a witness in criminal proceedings.

of the process of work with children and families. The timescales and procedures for reviewing plans for children in need which are also part of other guidance, regulations and legislation (child protection plans, care plans for children looked after and pathway plans) are already prescribed. For children in need plans, where work is being undertaken to support children and families in the community, it is good practice to review the plan with family members **at least every six months**, and to formally record it. Key professionals should also be involved in the review process and in constructing the revised plan.

4.37 The purpose of an assessment is to identify the child's needs within their family context and to use this understanding to decide how best to address these needs. It is essential that the plan is constructed on the basis of the findings from the assessment and that this plan is reviewed and refined over time to ensure the agreed case objectives are achieved. Specific outcomes for the child, expressed in terms of their health and development can be measured. These provide objective evidence against which to evaluate whether the child and family have been provided with appropriate services and ultimately whether the child's wellbeing is optimal.

5

Roles and Resposibilities in Inter-Agency Assessment of Children in Need

Principles of Inter-Disciplinary and Inter-Agency Assessment

5.1 A key principle of the Assessment Framework is that children's needs and their families circumstances will require inter-agency collaboration to ensure full understanding of what is happening and to ensure an effective service response. This chapter elaborates further on the roles and responsibilities of different disciplines and agencies when assessing whether a child is in need under the Children Act 1989. Some children in need may be being assessed concurrently under legislation other than the Children Act 1989. Other children may have already been assessed under different legislation and may be in receipt of services from agencies but not from social services. A further group of children may have parents or other significant family members or caregivers who are in receipt of social services.

5.2 In order to ensure optimal outcomes for children, whilst at the same time avoiding duplication of services or children receiving no service at all, it is important for all disciplines and agencies to work in a co-ordinated way to an agreed plan. Increasingly, there are service developments designed on a multi-agency basis, where teams operate with a pooled budget and shared objectives. An example is Youth Offending Teams.

5.3 There may be a number of voluntary and private organisations and community based groups, whose staff and volunteers have knowledge of a child and their family. In undertaking an assessment, it is important to find appropriate ways of using their understanding of the family to inform the overall analysis of the child's needs and how best to help the family. Communication with staff and volunteers from other agencies and groups should be based on the principles of confidentiality and consent set out in paragraphs 3.46 to 3.57.

5.4 Inter-agency, inter-disciplinary assessment practice requires an additional set of knowledge and skills to that required for working within a single agency or independently. It requires that all staff understand the roles and responsibilities of staff working in contexts different to their own. Having an understanding of the perspectives, language and culture of other professionals can inform how communication is conducted. This prevents professionals from misunderstanding one another because they use different language to describe similar concepts or because they are influenced by stereotypical perceptions of the other discipline. The use of the Assessment Framework for assessing children in need provides a language which is common to children and their family members, as well as to professionals and other staff.

Corporate Responsibilities for Children in Need

5.5 Under s17 of the Children Act 1989, social services departments carry lead responsibility for establishing whether a child is in need and for ensuring services are provided to that child as appropriate. This may not require social services to provide the service itself. Following a child in need assessment, for example, a child with communication impairment may require the help of a NHS speech therapist and additional classroom support at school rather than any specialist services of the social services department. The voluntary sector may have an important role to play in contributing to an assessment and providing services to a family.

5.6 This inter-agency responsibility is spelt out in s17(5) of the Children Act 1989.

> *Every local authority –*
>
> a *shall facilitate the provision by others (including in particular voluntary organisations) of services which the authority have power to provide by virtue of this section, or section 18, 20, 23 or 24; and*
>
> b *may make such arrangements as they see fit for any person to act on their behalf in the provision of any such service.*
>
> Children Act 1989 s17(5)

5.7 The corporate responsibilities for working with children in need and their families have been emphasised in the Government's objectives for children's social services (Department of Health, 1999e).

> The Government believes that local authorities corporately have a responsibility to address the needs of such children and young people. There should be effective joint working by education, housing and leisure in partnership with social services and health. Social services alone cannot promote the social inclusion and development of these children and families. However, in partnership with others, social services can play a vital role (p.4).

Inter-Agency Responsibilities for Assessments of Children in Need

5.8 The next section sets out the responsibilities of local authority departments and health authorities for assessing children in need and their families and the basis on which professionals working in statutory agencies and independent settings work with social services staff who have lead responsibility for this task. This section should be read in conjunction with Chapter 3 in *Working Together to Safeguard Children* (1999) which addresses the primary roles and responsibilities of statutory agencies, professionals, the voluntary and private sector and the wider community in respect of children, and in particular children about whom there is concern that they may be suffering or are suffering significant harm. The following sections address specifically some of the key issues about agency roles and responsibilities when assessing children in need or contributing to other assessments of children and their families. It includes most of the major agencies but is not comprehensive.

Social Services Departments

5.9 The social services department has the lead role for ensuring initial and core assessments are carried out according to the *Framework for the Assessment of Children in Need and their Families*. In practice this means, planning, preparation, co-ordination and communication with professionals in other agencies, in accordance with the principles set out in paragraph 1.23. This is where inter-agency protocols (and intra-agency where adults services are concerned) can be an effective means of providing a structure for collaboration and lines of communication.

5.10 With any child or family referral, social services should check whether the person with parenting responsibility has needs independent of the child's needs, which may call for the provision of adult community care services. If so, those needs should be further assessed in accordance with *Achieving Fairer Access to Adult Social Care Services* (Department of Health, forthcoming, a). The assessment of the child's needs and the capacity of their parent(s) to respond appropriately to those needs within their family context, should follow the *Framework for the Assessment of Children in Need and their Families*.

5.11 With any adult referral, social services should check whether the person has parenting responsibility for a child under 18. If so, the initial assessment should explore any parenting and child related issues in accordance with the *Framework for the Assessment of Children in Need and their Families*. This will determine if the child is in need, and the nature of services required to support his or her family, under Section 17 of the Children Act 1989. Further assessment should be undertaken and services provided as appropriate, following this Guidance. The assessment of adult needs should follow the *Achieving Fairer Access to Adult Social Care Services Guidance*.

5.12 Where the child is looked after or there is concern about significant harm, the responsibilities of local authorities are clearly laid out in *Children Act 1989 Guidance and Regulations* (1991) and in *Working Together to Safeguard Children* (1999). Although social services will continue to work closely with other agencies in such circumstances, it is social services which has a statutory duty to safeguard and promote the welfare of children and to ensure that this is effectively carried out.

5.13 The role of the key worker for a child whose name has been placed on a Child Protection Register is set out in paragraph 5.76 of *Working Together to Safeguard Children* (1999). It states that the key worker has responsibility for completing the core assessment of the child and family and securing contributions from core group members and others as necessary.

5.14 For children looked after and children whose names have been placed on the child protection register and who are subject to a child protection plan, the responsibilities for monitoring and reviewing the children's progress (including safety) are set out in the same *Regulations and Guidance* (Department of Health 1991; Department of Health *et al*, 1999). Social services departments have lead responsibility for ensuring these reviews take place within the prescribed time scales. As stated in Chapter 4, there are no such regulations governing the review of welfare of other children in need. However, it is essential that agreements are reached on an inter-agency basis about how best to monitor and review children in need plans. The lead agency for this activity may not necessarily be the social services department, as another agency may be better placed to undertake this responsibility.

5.15 In the process of all relevant agencies working collaboratively to construct and agree the child in need plan, decisions will have been made about which agencies will provide the necessary services. Careful thought should be given to which professional would be best placed to have lead responsibility for co-ordinating the review of the child in need plan. Amongst the considerations will be the respective roles and responsibilities of the various agencies.

Voluntary and Independent Agencies

5.16 Voluntary and independent agencies are key providers of a number of different types of services for children and families. They may be undertaking or contributing to assessments for a range of purposes: under the terms of a service agreement with a social services department, in partnership with other agencies or organisations or as part of the service they provide in response to direct referrals from children and families. Their staff's knowledge and use of the Assessment Framework when undertaking an assessment will enable information to be organised within a common framework, using a common language. This will be particularly important where the assessment has been commissioned by a social services department.

Health Authority

5.17 Every Health Authority is required to work with local agencies and trusts to consider the health needs of their residents and then determine local priorities and ways to address those needs. In particular Health Authorities and Primary Care Groups and Trusts should ensure that they participate in inter-agency planning and co-operation through Children's Services Plans and Quality Protects Management Action Plans, and that there are clear cross references in the Health Improvement Programmes.

5.18 The Health Improvement Programme is a jointly agreed health strategy which has the support of the local authority, NHS Trusts and Primary Care Groups. Services for healthcare for vulnerable children should be described and the health authority should ensure that local services and professionals contribute fully and effectively to local inter-agency working to safeguard children and promote their welfare.

5.19 The Health Authority should agree with Primary Care Groups and Trusts (PCG/Ts) how the local health service obligation to contribute to assessments involving inter-agency working should be discharged locally. Service specifications drawn up by PCG/Ts should include clear service standards for assessments of children in need. For children where there are grounds for concern that they are suffering significant harm these must be consistent with local Area Child Protection Committee protocols.

5.20 NHS Trusts and PCG/Ts are responsible for providing acute and community health services in hospital and community settings, and a wide range of staff will come into contact with children and parents in the course of their normal duties. Staff should be alert to concerns about a child's health and development and should know how to act upon these concerns in line with local protocols. Conversely, they should also be aware of how adult patients with, for example, physical or mental illness may require help to carry out their parent roles successfully.

5.21 Most health professionals, in the NHS, private sector, and other agencies play an important part in the lives of children and their parents. Because of the universal nature of health provision, health professionals are often the first to become aware of the needs of children or that some families are experiencing difficulties looking after their children. They should consider what help would benefit those families. Social services departments can assist health professionals by providing information about help that is available in the community and through their own departments.

The General Practitioner and the Primary Health Care Team

5.22 The General Practitioner (GP) and other members of the primary health care team (PHCT) are well placed to recognise when a child is potentially in need of extra support or services to promote health and development, or may be at risk of suffering significant harm. Primary care team members should know when it is appropriate to refer a child, as a potential child in need, to social services for help and support, and how to act on concerns that a child may be at risk of harm through abuse or neglect. When other members of the primary care team become concerned about the welfare of a child, the GP should be involved in discussing these concerns. The GP and primary health care team will have an important contribution to make to initial and core assessments of children in need.

5.23 The GP and the primary health care team are also well placed to recognise when a parent or other adult has problems which may affect their capacity as a parent or carer, or which may mean that they pose a risk of harm to a child. While GPs have responsibilities to all their patients, the child is particularly vulnerable and the welfare of the child of paramount importance. If they have concerns that an adult's problems or behaviour may be causing, or putting a child at risk of harm, they should follow the procedures set out in *Working Together to Safeguard Children* (1999).

Nurses, Midwives, Health Visitors and School Nurses

5.24 Nurses work in a variety of settings where they are likely to meet vulnerable children and their families. They will consider the circumstances in which it would be appropriate to refer them to social services departments for further assessment. They will then continue to work in partnership with social workers, general practitioners and others to contribute to integrated assessments, through sharing facts and professional opinions and by helping children and families identify and address their own needs.

5.25 The midwife and health visitor are uniquely placed to identify risk factors to a child during pregnancy, birth and the child's early care. Health visitors and school nurses monitor child health, growth and physical, emotional and social development. In addition, health visitors are aware of the health of the parents and may identify particular difficulties, for example, postnatal depression in mothers. The regular contact health visitors and school nurses have with children and families gives them an important role to play in the promotion of children's health and development and the protection of children from harm. Many of these staff provide parental support services or parenting sessions and programmes. Some also offer leadership to local schemes which support parents.

Paediatric Services

5.26 If, in the course of a social services department assessments of children in need, an opinion from a specialist paediatric service (including child development teams which are multi-disciplinary and may include a social worker) is required, the service should be requested by or after consultation with the appropriate member of the Primary Health Care Team. Where an urgent opinion is required, because there are grounds for concern that a child is suffering significant harm, this should be sought in line with local child protection procedures.

5.27 A paediatrician and/or a child development team may already know a child who is being assessed by a social services department. This will certainly be the case for children with chronic or recurrent significant illnesses and for disabled children. Social workers based in child development teams should be guided by the Assessment Framework when preparing their contribution to a multi-disciplinary assessment of a disabled child and family. Health professionals seeing such a child will have a contribution to make both to an assessment of need and in advising on medical and child development services that would be of benefit to the child and family. Information should be shared with the informed consent of the parents and of the child (obtained in a way appropriate to the child's age and understanding).

5.28 Many paediatric services have an identified lead Community Paediatrician for children in need who can advise social workers and parents on how to gain access to services. Within the health services, community paediatricians can raise awareness of the difficulties faced by vulnerable and disadvantaged families. Innovations are being proposed (eg. within Health Action Zone schemes) for the introduction of one stop shops where social services and health staff can work together to provide supportive and therapeutic services for children and their families.

Professionals Allied to Health

5.29 Other professionals allied to health, for example audiologists, physiotherapists, occupational therapists and speech therapists will also have important roles to play in the lives of some disabled and developmentally delayed children. Of these professionals, speech therapists are the most likely to be involved in the assessment of children in need. This is because the language development of children is most often affected by adverse environmental and family circumstances. Speech and language therapists can also provide expertise to facilitate communication with a child during an assessment.

Mental Health Services

5.30 Mental health problems are relatively common in children. Preliminary results of a recent survey found that around 10 per cent of 5–15 year olds in England, Scotland and Wales has some type of mental disorder sufficient to cause considerable distress and substantial interference with personal functioning in most cases (Office for National Statistics, 1999). Children of families in Social Class V (unskilled occupations) were about three times as likely to have a mental health problem compared with those in Social Class I (professionals). There are strong associations between family income and the mental health of children.

5.31 The evident increased likelihood of children in need having a significant mental health problem indicates the importance of specific consideration being given to their mental health needs. Not all children and young people, however, will require the help of specialists and, for many, effective and straightforward interventions at an early stage may prevent more serious problems developing later.

5.32 Those children and young people with more severe and complex disorders will require both specialist services and community based support to ensure the best possible outcomes. Social workers and other staff working within such services, whether in hospital or community child and family mental health service settings, should draw on knowledge of the Assessment Framework to inform their contributions.

5.33 An assessment of the mental health of a child or young person will attempt to unravel the various factors that have played a part in the causation of any particular problem or difficulty. This will include an assessment of those factors that are protective as well as those that constitute a risk to the child. As understanding about the aetiology of mental disorders in children increases, it is clear that attention must be given as much to intrinsic factors in the child, such as inherited temperamental characteristics, as to the external social and family influences. This is particularly relevant for children with hyperkeinetic disorder, for instance, whose parents otherwise might feel totally responsible for their child's difficult, demanding and hyperactive behaviour.

5.34 Child and adolescent mental health services provide a range of psychiatric and psychological assessment and treatment services for children and families. There may be very specific reasons why a specialist child mental health professional may become involved. The possibility of a psychotic illness (eg. schizophrenia), suicide or risk of self harm, the consideration of medical or psychological treatment for hyperkeinetic disorder or attention deficit hyperactivity disorder (ADHD), attachment disorders and an assessment of post traumatic stress following severe trauma are all clear cut examples. A referral may also be made for an assessment of individual family factors which contribute to a child's disorder and to ascertaining the therapeutic needs of the child and family members. Many requests, however, are less specific and these often relate to the complexity and chronicity of problems experienced by children who have suffered from a variety of disadvantages and adversities. Assessments of aggressive and oppositional behaviour of a child, family functioning, parenting capacity, and attachment between parent and child are other examples of important mental health tasks where child and mental health services might usefully contribute. In these circumstances a consultation or planning session may help clarify who is best able to undertake which task and what types of intervention may be most appropriate to help the child and family.

5.35 Some children and young people may require admission to hospital for psychiatric treatment. The legal framework governing the admission to hospital and treatment of children is complex. The use and relevance of the Mental Health Act 1983 or the Children Act 1989 should be considered particularly where consent is an issue. Professionals charged with responsibility for helping the child will use the statutory framework which reflects the predominant needs of the child. *The Mental Health Act 1983 Code of Practice* (Department of Health and the Welsh Office, 1999) contains essential guidance (see in particular chapter 31) which should inform the assessment and treatment of children who are either formal or informal patients.

5.36 Adult mental health services, including those providing general adult and community, forensic, psychotherapy, alcohol and substance misuse and learning disability services, have a key role to play in the assessment process when parental problems in these areas have an impact on their capacity to respond appropriately to their children's needs (see paragraphs 6.18 to 6.22 on commissioning specialist services). *Crossing Bridges* (Falkov (ed), 1998) was developed to help staff working with mentally ill parents and their children. It provides a rich source of training material for both adult and children's services staff.

5.37 There are two specific pieces of guidance regarding children visiting parents, other family members and close friends in psychiatric settings where social services departments may be asked to assess whether it is in the best interests of a child to visit a named patient.

5.38 *The Visits by Children to Ashworth, Broadmoor and Rampton Hospital Authorities Directions* (HSC 1999/160) and the *Guidance to Local Authority Social Services Departments on Visits by Children to Special Hospitals* (LAC(99)23) sets out the assessment process to be followed when deciding whether a child can visit a named patient in these hospitals. When a social services department considers it has powers under the Children Act 1989 to undertake the necessary assessment, it is required to assist the hospital by assessing whether it is in the interests of a particular child to visit a named patient and providing the special hospital with this information.

5.39 The Circular *Mental Health Act 1983 Code of Practice: Guidance on the visiting of psychiatric patients by children* (HSC1999/222 LAC(99)32) sets out principles to underpin child-visiting policies in respect of children visiting patients in other psychiatric units. This guidance emphasises the importance of facilitating a child's contact especially with their parents or other key family members, wherever possible. Where there are child welfare concerns, the Trust may ask the social services department where the child is resident to assess whether it is in the best interests of a child to visit a named patient.

Psychologists

5.40 Psychologists – clinical, counselling, educational, forensic – who work with children and families are well placed to contribute to core assessments and to offer a range of services to support children in need and their families. In particular, educational psychologists working with children, their parents, schools and other agencies to promote children's social, emotional and intellectual development will have a significant contribution to make.

Education Services

5.41 A major protective factor in a child's life is having good relationships and succeeding in school. Education staff, through their day to day contact with pupils, have a crucial role to play enabling children to have positive experiences in school – academically and through good relationships – as well as ensuring and observing their wellbeing. Education Welfare Officers and Educational psychologists may, through their work with schools, have knowledge of a particular child. If a child is thought to be in need, social services departments may be able to assist. With parental agreement, these concerns may be discussed with the local social services department and a way forward agreed on identified matters.

5.42 Schools and colleges may on occasions be asked by a social services department for information about a child for whom there are concerns about their health or development, abuse or neglect. The education service itself does not have a direct investigative responsibility in child protection work, but schools and other maintained establishments have a role in assisting the social services department by referring concerns and providing information for s47 child protection enquiries. The role of the independent schools in relation to child protection is the same as that of any other school (Paragraphs 3.12 and 3.15 in *Working Together to Safeguard Children,* 1999).

5.43 When a child has special educational needs, or is disabled, schools and educational psychologists will have important information about the child's development, their level of understanding and the most effective means of communicating with the child. This information should be sought before beginning an assessment. The school and the educational psychologist will also be well placed to give a view on the impact of different types of treatment or intervention on the child's care or behaviour.

5.44 *Social Inclusion: Pupil Support* (Department for Education and Employment,1999a) sets out government guidance on pupil attendance, behaviour, exclusion and re-integration of children at school. It takes a multi-agency approach to supporting schools and enabling them to help pupils with behavioural difficulties, including poor attendance. Where a pupil may be at serious risk of permanent exclusion from school or engaging in criminal activity, a **Pastoral Support Programme** should be set up to plan interventions to help the pupil remain in school. The social services department should as appropriate be involved in the programme (see paragraph 5.5 of Circular 10/99). In addition to contributing to work undertaken with pupils by staff from other agencies, social services departments can assist directly by working with individual children and their families who are experiencing difficulties which impact on the child's educational progress. This could include work with children who are caring for a sick or disabled adult, or where there are relationship difficulties within the family, or where a child has suffered abuse or neglect. In such situations where a child and family is referred to a social services department for help with difficulties identified at school, an initial assessment will be undertaken using the dimensions in the Assessment Framework to ascertain if the child is in need and what help could be offered to respond to the particular needs of the child and their family.

5.45 **Children looked after** can experience a range of problems at school due to the disruptions experienced prior to and during care. These disruptions often include breaks in education. Good liaison with **schools** is important, both to ascertain the school's assessment of these young people and their current needs and to plan with the school how these needs can best be met. *Guidance on the Education of Children and Young People in Public Care* (Department for Education and Employment and Department of Health, forthcoming) sets out the importance of education to young people in public care and the action that local authorities (education and social services departments) must take to safeguard the education and thus the future of these young people.

5.46   **Learning Mentors** are a new resource, being introduced in secondary schools in major cities as part of the Government's Excellence in Cities initiative. They will work closely with pupils to help them to overcome barriers to learning. They will provide intensive counselling and support to a small number of pupils facing significant problems, and will perform a 'signposting' function for others, helping them to access other agencies and local systems of support, such as business and community mentoring schemes and social services. It will be important for learning mentors to work closely with local social services departments in supporting the pupils in their charge.

5.47   Part of the learning mentor function is to participate in progress checks for pupils in year 7 and year 9. They will also draw up individual targets for the pupil to achieve at school. Each school will have its own assessment arrangements in place for progress checks, but all learning mentors will be informed about the Assessment Framework, and encouraged to use a consistent format in order to facilitate effective information sharing.

5.48   The Connexions strategy (Department for Education and Employment, 2000) will introduce a universal network of Personal Advisers for young people. The **Connexions Service** will seek to develop a common assessment tool, with a common core and sections related to specific problems a young person might face, that can be used by all Personal Advisers to assess a young person's needs. Its use will allow different agencies to agree on how a young person's needs can be met either directly or through referral, and encourage a co-ordinated response to a young person's needs. The development of this assessment tool will take full account of this framework for assessing children in need.

5.49   For most young people, the end of compulsory education (at around the age of 16) marks a significant decision and transition point in their development towards adulthood. Government maintained schools have a legal duty to prepare children for this decision and transition by providing a programme of careers education and guidance during the last three years of their compulsory education. Various assessment methods are used to help children identify their occupational interests and potential. The methods include self-assessment questionnaires, standardised tests and practical tasks which are formally assessed.

5.50   In 1999 the Department for Education and Employment established a new form of provision for young people who had failed to make a successful transition from compulsory education. This programme – known as the Learning Gateway – is run jointly by careers services and Training and Enterprise Councils. Personal advisers help 16 and 17 year olds who are struggling to find their way to identify realistic career goals and to obtain a suitable learning or employment opportunity. This often involves some remedial education/preparatory training in basic skills and personal effectiveness before the young person is ready for mainstream provision. The Department for Education and Employment has provided comprehensive *Guidance on Assessment in the Learning Gateway* (Department for Education and Employment, 1999b). This covers both vocational assessment and the assessment of pre-vocational learning and development needs such as personal effectiveness and social skills.

5.51   **Youth and Community Workers** have close contact with young people. They should be alert to any concerns about a young person's welfare and know how to refer to the social services department if they consider a child would benefit from its help. They will also be well placed to assist in a child in need assessment. In some instances joint working may be appropriate.

Special Educational Needs Code of Practice

5.52 Education legislation does not distinguish between disability and special educational needs. Not all children with special educational needs have a disability. Equally some disabled children do not have special educational needs. In January 1999, schools in England identified 20% (1.52 million) of their pupils as having some form of special educational needs, and 3% (248,000) of pupils had statements of Special Educational Needs.

5.53 Special educational needs cover a wide spectrum of needs/difficulties including emotional and behavioural difficulties which are described within the code as:

- Emotional and behavioural difficulties may result, for example, from abuse or neglect; physical or mental illness; sensory or physical impairment; or psychological trauma. In some cases emotional and behavioural difficulties may arise from, or be exacerbated by, circumstances within the school environment. They may also be associated with other learning difficulties.

- Emotional and behavioural difficulties may become apparent in a wide variety of forms – including withdrawal, depressive or suicidal attitudes; obsessional pre-occupations with eating habits; school phobia; substance misuse; disruptive, antisocial and unco-operative behaviour; and frustration, anger and threat of actual violence (*Special Educational Needs Code of Practice*, paragraphs 3.65 and 3.66).

5.54 Under the Education Act 1996, local education authorities have a duty to identify and make a statutory assessment of those children for whom they are responsible who have special educational needs and who probably require a statement of their special educational needs. A child is said to have **special educational needs** if (s)he has:

A learning difficulty which calls for special educational provision to be made for him

5.55 A child has a learning difficulty if:

> a. *he has a significantly greater difficulty in learning than the majority of children his age;*
>
> b. *he has a disability which either prevents or hinders him from making use of educational facilities of a kind generally provided for children of his age in schools within the area of the LEA, or*
>
> c. *he is under the age of five and is, or would be if special educational provision were not made for him, likely to fall within paragraph (a) or (b) when over that age.*

5.56 Having decided that a statutory assessment should be made, the local education authority must seek parental, educational, medical, psychological and the social services department's advice. Where a child is known to a social services department, the social worker should draw on information which has already been gathered and is on the child's file. At the same time, the social services department may decide to undertake a child in need assessment under s17 of the Children Act 1989, to ascertain whether social services would benefit the child and family.

5.57 The *Code of Practice on the Identification and Assessment of Special Educational Practice* (1994) sets out the duties of health authorities and social services departments in respect of children who may have special educational needs as follows:

> All those bodies to which the Code applies must, of course, fulfil their duties. But it is up to them to decide how to do so, in the light of the guidance in the Code of Practice. All those to whom the Code applies have a statutory duty to have regard to it; they must not ignore it. Whenever the health services and social services help schools and LEAs take action on behalf of such children those bodies must consider what the Code says.

5.58 When a statement of special educational needs has been completed, the social services department will be provided with a copy of the statement and the accompanying advice from professionals. This information can assist social services in current or future work with the child and family.

Day Care Services

5.59 Day care services – family centres, early years centres, nurseries (including workplace nurseries), childminders, playgroups and holiday and out of school schemes – play an increasingly important part in the lives of growing numbers of children. Many services will be offering a range of support to children and families experiencing problems and stress. This makes them well placed to intervene early and resolve difficulties before they become more serious or entrenched.

5.60 Day care services may identify children where there are concerns about their developmental progress or wellbeing, or alternatively parents who may have difficulties in responding to their child's needs sufficiently or appropriately. Day care services may contribute by:

- identifying and referring families to social services departments;

- contributing to the assessment of children and their parents or caregivers, sometimes providing a specialist assessment of family relationships;

- providing services which support the child's development and strengthen the parents' capacity to respond, through routine work or as part of a child care plan which is monitored and reviewed.

Sure Start

5.61 **Sure Start** is an area based programme providing universal services for children under four and their families in some of the most disadvantaged communities. Sure Start aims to improve the health and wellbeing of children and families before and from birth, so children are ready to thrive and succeed when they go to school.

5.62 Local programmes work with parents and parents-to-be to improve the life chances of young children through better access to:

- family support;

- advice on nurturing;

- health services;

- early learning.

5.63 Sure Start programmes provide a range of co-ordinated services, locally determined, to meet national objectives and targets and local priorities. These are likely to include:

- outreach and home visiting;

- support for families and parents;

- support for good quality play, learning and childcare experiences for children;

- primary and community health care, including advice about family health and child health and development;

- support for children and parents with special needs, including help accessing specialised services.

5.64 Sure Start programmes are run by local partnerships bringing together people from statutory agencies, voluntary and community organisations and local parents to plan and organise local services. The involvement of local parents in Sure Start partnerships ensures that services are responsive to local needs and will strengthen local communities, and build capacity and confidence.

5.65 Sure Start provides an opportunity for early support and intervention and to ensure that health, education and social services are actively engaged in supporting the most vulnerable pre-school children. Some children and families using Sure Start services may be referred to or known to social services departments as children in need. Co-ordinated assessments will therefore be essential as part of providing effective services to secure optimal outcomes.

Youth Offending Teams

5.66 The principal aim of the youth justice system, to prevent offending by children and young people, is set out in the Crime and Disorder Act 1998. Under this Act, the Local Authority, acting in co-operation with every chief officer of police and police authority and every probation committee and health authority in the local authority's area, has a duty to *secure that, to such extent as is appropriate for their area, all youth justice services are available there* (s38) and that a Youth Offending Team is in place (s40) comprising police and probation officers, social workers and education and health staff. The Youth Offending Teams (YOTs), which are multi-agency, have responsibility for co-ordinating or delivering the provision of local youth justice services and helping to implement the Youth Justice Plan (s41).

5.67 The Youth Justice Board for England and Wales has developed an assessment profile, ASSET, for use with all youth offenders who enter and leave the youth justice system. ASSET provides YOTs with a consistent means of assessing the needs of individual young people and the risks of their re-offending, causing harm to themselves or to others. The profile covers the areas of a young person's life most linked to offending behaviour including living arrangements, family and personal relationships, education, employment and training, lifestyle, substance use, physical health, emotional and mental health, personal identity and cognitive and behavioural development. In addition, there is a detailed risk of harm assessment for use when the profile suggests that the young offender has the potential to commit serious harm to others. The profile will assist practitioners plan a programme of interventions to meet the identified needs of the young person and reduce the factors associated with risks of re-offending, causing harm to themselves or to others.

5.68   It will be important for YOTs completing ASSET to liaise within social services departments about young people with whom social services have had or have contact. Prior assessments of need undertaken by social services departments can inform the work of YOTs. Similarly, assessments undertaken by YOTs will be an important source of knowledge if the young person continues to be worked with as a child in need under the Children Act 1989 or is re-referred to the social services department for help following their involvement with the youth justice system. The dimensions of the Assessment Framework in this Guidance are consistent with those of the youth offending assessment profile. The key difference is that ASSET concentrates in depth on areas of a young person's life most likely to be associated with offending behaviour.

Housing

5.69   Housing Authority staff, through their day to day contact with members of the public, may become aware of concerns about the welfare of particular children and should refer to one of the statutory agencies as appropriate.

5.70   Equally, Housing Authorities may have important information about families which could be helpful to social services departments carrying out assessments under s17 or s47 of the Children Act 1989. In accordance with their duty to assist under s27 of the Children Act 1989, they should be prepared to share relevant information verbally or in writing, including attending child protection conferences when requested to do so.

5.71   The provision of appropriate housing can make an important contribution to meeting the health and developmental needs of children. Housing Authorities should be prepared to assist in the provision of accommodation, either directly, through their links with other housing providers or by the provision of advice.

5.72   Social services departments have a duty under section 20(3) of the Children Act 1989 to accommodate any child in need aged 16 and 17 whose welfare is likely to be seriously prejudiced without the provision of accommodation. At the same time, Housing Authorities are required under the Housing Act 1996 to secure accommodation for people who are homeless, eligible for assistance and in priority need. Homeless young people may frequently come to the notice of both housing and social services and will need to be assessed to establish whether they should be provided with accommodation. There is a danger that in these circumstances young people may be passed from one agency to another and it is important therefore that joint protocols are agreed between housing and social services in the matter of how and by whom they are to be assessed.

Police

5.73   The role of members of the Police Force can be seen quite broadly in terms of the overall wellbeing and welfare of children and their families. They have a key role in their knowledge of local communities. Information may be available from the police either generally about local environmental factors or specifically about family or household members. Their contribution in referring children and families to social services departments and in providing information and advice should be considered when undertaking a child in need assessment. The role of the police in relation to safeguarding children is set out in paragraphs 3.57 to 3.64 of *Working Together to Safeguard Children* (1999).

5.74 Protecting life and preventing crime are primary tasks of the police. Children are citizens who have the right to the protection offered by the criminal law. The police have a duty and responsibility to investigate criminal offences committed against children, and such investigations should be carried out sensitively, thoroughly and professionally. The police should be notified as soon as possible where a criminal offence has been committed, or is suspected of being committed, against a child.

5.75 The police have a responsibility to co-ordinate and lead the risk assessment and management process for the exchange of information about all those who have been convicted of, cautioned for, or otherwise dealt with by the courts for a sexual offence; and those who are considered to present a risk to children and others (see paragraphs 7.37 and 7.38 of *Working Together to Safeguard Children* (1999)).

Probation Services

5.76 Probation Services have a statutory duty to supervise offenders effectively in order to reduce offending and protect the public. In the execution of that duty, probation services will be in contact with, or supervising, a number of men (and, to a far lesser extent, women) who have convictions for offences against children. When undertaking assessments of children in need social services staff should draw on the knowledge probation services have about family members or other adults in contact with a child and family, who may have committed offences against children.

5.77 The Probation Service has an important role in working with men and women in prison who may be parents of children under the age of 18. Probation should be informed by social services if an assessment of a child whose parent is in prison is being undertaken and should be asked to contribute. There may be a range of issues when a parent is in prison which will need careful assessment and planning, for example, contact between parent and child; reunification and release arrangements; resettlement in the community. Joint working between probation and social services may be essential to securing the wellbeing of the child.

5.78 In addition, specialist probation officers working in the family courts may be alerted to child care concerns through their investigations as court welfare officers, for example, through work with families under Family Assistance Orders (s16 of the Children Act 1989).

The Prison Service

5.79 The Prison Service works closely with other agencies to identify any prisoner who may represent a risk to the public on release. Regular risk assessment takes account of progress made during the sentence, and informs decisions on sentence planning for individual prisoners, including sex offender treatment programmes. Governors are required to notify social services departments and the probation service of plans to release prisoners convicted of offences against children and young people so that appropriate action can be taken by agencies in the community to minimise any risk to children or young people (Instruction to Governors 54/1994).

5.80 The Prison Service has a duty to safeguard the welfare of those children aged under 18 in its custody. From 1 April 2000, all Prison Service Establishments in the new under 18 estate are required to appoint a child protection co-ordinator; and to establish, in consultation with local ACPCs, arrangements for acting on allegations or concerns that a young person may have suffered, or is at risk of suffering significant harm (HM Prison Service, 2000). A s47 enquiry and core assessment is undertaken concurrently drawing on knowledge of the Assessment Framework.

5.81 When a young person is entering or leaving a Young Offender Institution or prison, it will be important for there to be close liaison between staff in the prison service and the social services department, regarding children already known to a social services department or who are considered likely to benefit from the provision of social services assistance on their release.

5.82 The Prison Service may ask a social services department to carry out an assessment regarding a baby whose mother is in prison (HM Prison Service, 1999). This may be to assist the Service decide whether it is in the best interests of a baby to live with his or her mother in a mother and baby unit. In rare instances, it may be as part of the process of making s47 enquiries where there are concerns about the safety of a child who is living with his or her mother in a mother and baby unit. Mother and baby units are not a place of safety. A prison governor may refer children to a social services department if she or he believe the baby is at risk with the identified carer or other adults.

Armed Services

5.83 In England, social services departments have statutory responsibility for safeguarding and promoting the welfare of children of Services families. When Services families (or civilians working with the Armed Forces) are based overseas, the responsibility for their welfare is vested with the Ministry of Defence. All three Services provide professional welfare support and in some cases, medical support, to augment those provided by local authorities.

5.84 When social services departments are undertaking assessments of children in need, contact should be made with the welfare service appropriate to the particular Service. Appendix 2 of *Working Together to Safeguard Children* (1999) gives details of these Services and contact numbers. The roles and responsibilities of the Armed Forces in respect of safeguarding children of Services families or of ex-Services families are set out in paragraphs 3.89 to 3.96 of *Working Together to Safeguard Children* (1999).

Summary

5.85 This chapter has elaborated the roles and responsibilities of a range of agencies, organisations and disciplines that work with children and families. Understanding these roles and responsibilities is a cornerstone of effective inter-agency, inter-disciplinary working. Individual practitioners will use their professional relationships and networks to assist them achieve good outcomes for children and their families. Quality collaboration at an inter-personal level requires effective organisational arrangements to support these informal processes and ensure good inter-agency working is not solely dependent on the commitment of dedicated individuals.

6

Organisational Arrangements to Support Effective Assessment of Children in Need

6.1 This chapter considers the organisational arrangements which should be in place to support effective practice in assessing children in need and their families. A key longer term measure of success of the Assessment Framework will be evidence of improving outcomes for children as described in the Government's Objectives for Children's Social Services (Department of Health, 1999e). Another measure is whether the timescales set out in the objectives for undertaking initial and core assessments and responding to referrals are met. Chief Executives of local authorities have overall responsibility for ensuring that all departments of their authority play their part in achieving these objectives (Department of Health and Department for Education and Employment, 1999).

Government's Objectives for Children's Social Services

6.2 The *White Paper Modernising Social Services* (Department of Health, 1998e) set out the Government's objectives for both children's and adults' social services, together with objectives common to both on user involvement and training. A consolidated version of the Government's objectives for children's social services, incorporating more detailed sub-objectives, targets and performance indicators was published in September 1999. They outline the social services role, and what they are expected to achieve together with other agencies in the community for some of society's most disadvantaged families and most vulnerable children. This and other work has made clear that targeted help is required to ensure that disadvantaged children and young people are able to take maximum advantage of universal services – in particular education and health – as well as any specialist services.

6.3 In addition to working with children requiring support from social services, the Government believes that local authorities have a corporate responsibility to address the needs of a wider group of disadvantaged children, defined as children at risk of social exclusion. These are children who would benefit from extra help from public agencies in order to make the best of their life chances. To this end, there should be effective joint working by education, social services, housing, leisure and health. Social services alone cannot promote the social inclusion and development of these children and families. However, as part of a corporate endeavour, in partnership with others, social services can play a vital role.

6.4 Local authorities have to work closely with the NHS to ensure that shared objectives for children's services – particularly in areas such as services for disabled children and child and adolescent mental health services – are delivered effectively. The targets for child welfare in *Modernising Health and Social Services : National Priorities Guidance* (Department of Health, 1999j) are incorporated into the Government's objectives for children's social services.

6.5 A comprehensive performance assessment system based on the Best Value regime has been put into place to monitor the delivery of all social services and progress towards the objectives, priorities and targets set out by the Government. This includes in-year monitoring information, end-year performance data and in-depth evaluation through inspections and Joint Reviews. A set of 50 performance indicators were confirmed in July 1999 after a wide-ranging consultation exercise and 13 of these were designated statutory Best Value performance indicators in December 1999. Baseline data for 35 of the indicators were published in *Social Services Performance in 1998–99* (Department of Health, 1999k).

6.6 Elected members have a vital role in ensuring that the corporate responsibilities of local authorities are carried out. This was emphasised in a joint Department of Health/Local Government Association communication to local government councillors:

> As a councillor, you need to be involved in setting strategic objectives for children's services and monitoring how health care, education and life chances are improving for children who are looked after by your council, or who are in need of support in your community (Department of Health and the Local Government Association, 1999).

6.7 Good partnerships with the voluntary and private sector are also important to the delivery of the Government's objectives. In children's services, voluntary and private organisations are important providers of services. In addition to the family based services they already provide, they have a role in representing the voice of service users and carers, and in developing new and flexible approaches to service delivery. Local authorities should make sure that such organisations are fully involved in implementing the Assessment Framework.

6.8 Good assessment of the needs of children and families plays an important part in meeting the Government's children's social services objectives, by enabling needs to be identified at an early stage, so that services and support can be provided before problems escalate. *The Framework for the Assessment of Children in Need and their Families* will assist all agencies in making judgements about which children are in need and how best to help them.

Children's Services Planning

6.9 Children's Services Planning should provide the local vehicle for determining how the contributions of all the relevant agencies fit together and support each other in delivering shared objectives for vulnerable children and, in particular, children in need (Children's Services Planning Order, 1996). It is the Department of Health's intention to issue new guidance on planning for children's services which will address joint working towards these objectives.

6.10 A prime purpose of the children's services planning process is to ensure co-ordination and coherence across local planning arrangements for children and to improve the outcomes and efficiency of the services provided. Planning for children's services should ensure that local objectives in different plans are consistent and support each other. It is important to reduce duplication of planning effort. A balance has to be struck between ensuring that the separate policy intentions behind each set of plans are preserved and that planning is not carried out in separate compartments.

6.11 Fundamental to this will be effective information systems which identify the needs of local children and the nature of services required to meet those needs. Social services departments have an important contribution to make in this respect, in line with their responsibilities under the Children Act 1989:

> *Every local authority shall take reasonable steps to identify the extent to which there are children in need within their area.*
> **Children Act 1989, Schedule 2, Part 1, paragraph 1 (1).**

6.12 Record keeping and the aggregation of data from case records is a critical part of providing an information base for planning purposes. The assessment recording forms (Department of Health and Cleaver, 2000) have been designed to provide the means by which good quality data can be collected and aggregated by social services departments. They can be adapted for use by other agencies working with children, often the same children in need. A common recording system not only ensures data are collected in a consistent manner across agencies, but also facilitates communication about the particular needs of a child and about the needs of all children in an area.

6.13 These records will also provide a means by which supervisors and managers can monitor the quality of practitioners' work with children and families. They will enable them to monitor compliance in implementing the Assessment Framework. This monitoring is an integral part of the overall quality assurance process which departments should have in place.

Departmental Structures and Processes

6.14 The way in which a social service department is structured and the processes it uses to process requests for advice or information, referrals and further work with children and families should be organised to support staff responding to these requests and undertaking assessments of children in need within the required timescales. One example of how a department has organised itself was described in paragraph 3.6.

6.15 The formats for recording information about individual children and their families and the systems by which this information will be used for management and planning purposes will also make a significant contribution both to the effectiveness by which assessments of children in need can be undertaken and to the processes by which the appropriate services are planned and delivered in a local authority area, regionally and nationally.

Departmental Protocols and Procedures

6.16 Departmental procedures, and intra- and inter-agency protocols between adult's and children's services and between agencies involved in work with children and families respectively, which are consistent with the Assessment Framework, will facilitate working within social services departments and across agency boundaries. These should assist in reducing the amount of time spent on duplicated or unfocused work. These should not only benefit children and families but also achieve efficiency in this area and to contribute to **Best Value** in local government services.

6.17 It will be important to be explicit about expectations regarding staff having knowledge of and using the Assessment Framework when partnership arrangements, which include undertaking assessments, are being agreed between agencies. Similarly, when service level agreements are being drawn up, it will be essential for the social services department to be clear about it's expectations regarding the use of the Assessment Framework when, for example, a voluntary or independent agency is undertaking a specific type of assessment with a child and family.

Commissioning Specialist Assessments

6.18 There will be circumstances, where a specialist assessment will be necessary to provide information to social services departments when they are undertaking a core assessment. This is in addition to information that would normally be available about a child from other agencies in the community or information that is known as a result of a previous or current assessment.

6.19 In deciding who to commission to undertake a particular specialist assessment, social services should be clear about what type of assessment is required, for what purpose, within what timescale and who or what agency/professional is best placed to undertake it. This careful planning of specialist assessments not only contributes to the quality of the individual child in need assessment but also to the effective use of available resources. Local inter-agency protocols should provide guidance about how to commission specialist assessments, and who will implement the decision(s).

6.20 When commissioning a specialist assessment, it is important to ask questions which are within the remit of the particular professional to answer. For example, when a parent is being treated for alcohol addiction, it is appropriate for a social services practitioner to ask for an adult psychiatric opinion on the likelihood of the parent being able to stop or reduce his or her drinking, and the impact of the parent's addiction on behaviour, but not necessarily to ask whether that parent is capable of responding appropriately to the child's needs. The adult psychiatrist may also be able to offer an opinion on whether the parent is likely to both engage in and benefit from treatment. This could include treatment for personality disorders or mental health problems, as well as alcohol addiction.

6.21 Another example may occur where there are issues of sex offending; a practitioner who is involved in assessing a child's situation may need to know how effective a treatment programme has been for a particular sex offender, and how that information will assist the assessment of the child in need. It will be essential to check out with the profes-sional who undertook the therapeutic work, the areas in which they consider they have expertise, and what questions the professionals they consider they are qualified to answer. Some may have an excellent understanding of child and family work; others may conceive of their role solely within an adult context.

6.22 When an agency is commissioned to undertake a specialist assessment, this should be undertaken as part of the overall assessment. The findings should be integrated into an analysis of the needs of the child and family. There should be clarity about who has responsibility for analysing these findings and taking action forward, as spelt out in Chapter 4.

A Competent Work Force

6.23 Effective delivery of the Assessment Framework is dependent on the capacity of the workforce to implement it and having the appropriate resources to support the work force. This capacity relates to having sufficient staff in place, who have the requisite knowledge, skills and confidence to undertake assessments. They must be able to make sound judgements about the needs of each child and how best to enable those caring for them to respond appropriately to their needs.

6.24 Staff using the Assessment Framework should continue to update their knowledge about the needs of children and the effectiveness of interventions. This is a continuing process but one which is essential to ensure that members of the workforce are able to deliver good quality practice.

6.25 Knowledge of the wider context of national policy and research should be supplemented by information about the needs of the local population. Feedback from the analysis of locally collected information about what is happening to children and the impact of each agency's contribution should inform future plans and methods of intervention. There will always be debate about how best to help children and their families. These debates and consequent decisions should be continually informed by local and national information on what works in producing the best possible outcomes for children.

Supervision of Practice

6.26 Staff who are in the front line of practice must be well supported by effective supervision. The concepts of practice supervision varies from discipline to discipline. However, the underlying importance of supervision applies to all disciplines and should include consideration of the impact of working with children and families under stress. As Bentovim and Bingley Miller (forthcoming) point out:

> Supervision of workers carrying out family assessment is essential, as the assessment can have far reaching effects on the planning of care and whether families can respond to children's needs within their time frames.

6.27 It is important that supervision addresses:

- the process of assessment;

- the timing and relevance of making a child and family assessment;

- practice which recognises the diversity of family lives, traditions and behaviours;

- information about the children and the parents or caregivers, and its analysis;

- what further information is needed and how it will be obtained;

- the need for any immediate action or services;

- the plan for work with the child and family, and allocation of resources;

- the provision of services or intervention and their likely impact on child and family members;

- involvement/contact with staff in other agencies;

- the review of progress, of earlier understanding of the child and family's situation and of the action/intervention plan.

6.28 Agencies should consider carefully, therefore, the expertise, experience, knowledge and professional confidence of those who undertake the critical task of supervision. Their learning needs will be of equal importance to those of the practitioners who carry out assessments.

Staff as Members of Learning Organisations

6.29 This Guidance has an expectation that staff who work directly with children and families and those who supervise and manage this work are knowledgeable, confident and able to exercise professional judgement. This includes senior managers who carry important responsibilities for determining policy and practice at local level, for developing appropriate inter-agency relationships, and for securing and allocating resources.

6.30 An evidence based approach to practice requires front line staff to reflect on what they are doing during assessment and planning, and to examine the impact of their interventions and services on outcomes for children and families. To keep up to date, therefore, continuing learning is essential. It is critical that staff are provided with opportunities for developing appropriate competencies commensurate with their responsibilities and for staff development, including further and post qualifying training.

6.31 A culture of individual staff learning can only exist successfully within an organisational context which values this activity. Individual staff are being required to adapt and respond to changing expectations. This has repercussions for the way in which agencies direct and support their staff. Research in related areas suggests the importance of:

- **coherence** throughout the organisation about the objectives of policy and practice changes being implemented, exemplified in departmental arrangements, systems and procedures;

- commitment to the changes being reflected in the **values and behaviour** of staff throughout the organisation;

- acknowledgement that new policy expectations require adaptation and change, and involve the whole organisation in a **learning process**.

6.32 In this respect, Pearn *et al* (1995) write:

> In a world that changes at an ever accelerating rate, some organisations survive and thrive and others stagnate and die. With ever faster change as a permanent fact of life for all kinds of organisations, there is a growing need to make intentional use of learning processes to help ensure that they continue not only to survive but also to thrive, by reacting effectively to whatever the future may bring, but also helping to shape that future. In this sense all organisations need to be learning organisations. Organisations which are not learning as fast as they could or should, and have not ensured that they continue to learn, risk becoming less effective, becoming unhealthy, and eventually ceasing to exist.

6.33 These considerations, if firmly embedded in the organisation arrangements will contribute to ensuring effective assessments of children in need.

Preparing the Ground for Training and Continuing Staff Development

6.34 The Department of Health commissioned training materials, *The Child's World: Assessing Children in Need* (NSPCC and University of Sheffield, 2000), to assist the understanding and use of the Assessment Framework. The materials were funded from the Training Support Programme and therefore were intended primarily for a social services audience but can be used in inter-agency training on assessing children in need. These training materials were also designed to be used as part of a continuing programme of staff development. They should be used in qualifying and post qualifying social work training especially in the programmes leading to the Post Qualifying Child Care Award. They should also be of relevance to candidates for the Level 3 NVQ 'Caring for Children and Young People'. The occupational standards for child care at post qualifying level, should enable managers in performance appraisal to identify the current competences of staff and their learning needs.

6.35 The full range of resources commissioned by the Department of Health to support the Assessment Framework has been described in Chapter 4 in the accompanying practice guidance (Department of Health, 2000a).

6.36 Agencies should ensure that all practitioners, managers and administrative staff involved with children, are familiar with and keep up to date with developments in relation to the Assessment Framework. This will involve a range of training and briefing methods as a continuing programme of action.

6.37 A list of training and staff development issues which should be regularly considered and reviewed is listed on page 88 (Figure 8).

6.38 Once introduced, use of the Assessment Framework should be monitored and evaluated. The messages of initial training may be ignored or forgotten as staff become preoccupied with more pressing concerns; some will need additional advice about how the various materials should be used and the recording forms completed. Supervisors and managers have a key role in checking that the framework is being used appropriately and effectively, and that findings from individual assessments are informing planning and service provision of children's services.

Figure 8 TRAINING AND STAFF DEVELOPMENT ISSUES

Training Issues

A training strategy team, in consultation with senior managers, should consider and review:

- who needs training
- what will be single agency/inter-agency
- how much training
- who will do it
- how it will be resourced

The purpose of training would be to ensure that key staff know:

- why they are using the Assessment Framework
- the knowledge which underpins it
- what to use
- when to use it
- how to use it
- how to evaluate their practice (or work)

Staff Development Issues

A training strategy team could also consider:

- what are the continuing staff development needs
- how can these best be addressed.

Summary

6.39 In summary, the following organisational arrangements should be in place to support the effective assessments of children in need:

- policies, intra- and inter-agency protocols and procedures;

- assessment processes;

- structures and other processes for referral, planning and provision of services;

- recording and management information systems;

- training and staff development opportunities for professional staff, trainers, carers and others including administrative staff;

- inter-agency training programmes;

- quality control/quality assurance systems;

- child and family involvement and feedback on the assessment processes;

- systems for obtaining feedback on the implementation programme and then on the training programmes established on a continuing basis.

6.40 These arrangements will need to be monitored and reviewed from time to time to ensure they reflect the most up to date legislation, policies, procedures and evidence based knowledge. In this way, use of the Assessment Framework will be dynamic and continue to draw on developments in a rapidly changing world.

Appendix

A

The Assessment Framework

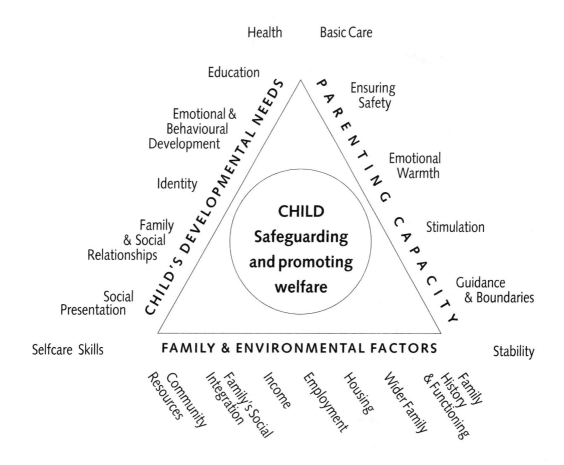

Appendix

A Framework for Analysing Services

THE ENABLING AUTHORITY

LEVEL OF INTERVENTION	WELFARE MODEL: ROLE OF STATE		
	Last resort: Safety net	Addressing Needs	Combatting Social disadvantages
Base (populations)			
First (vulnerable groups and communities: diversions)			Community development
Second (early stresses)		Social casework / Social care planning	
Third (severe stresses)	Remedial Interventions		
Fourth (social breakdown: 'in care'			

Reproduced with kind permission of the authors. From: Hardiker *et al* (1999) Children Still In Need, Indeed: prevention across five decades. In Stevenson O (1999) *Childhood Welfare in the UK*, p.43, Blackwell Science Ltd, Oxford.

 Referrals Involving a Child (Referral Chart)

Guide for use

This chart is designed to help you gather information at the initial referral stage. It is not exhaustive and should not be treated as a checklist. Please use the chart alongside the usual referral forms as a reminder of:

A. issues which may need to be checked

B. matters raised by the referrer that should be recorded.

What help is requested?

Material resources
Housing, beds, clothing, money, other

Practical help for parent/carer
Respite care, other

Support for parent/carer
Someone to talk to, advice/information, other

Support for child
Befriending, counselling, youth scheme, other

Support for referrer
Advice/information, discussion of current concern, other

Practical help for child
Accommodation, school place, specialist equipment, other

Protection for child
Home visit, immediate shelter, other

Is there a child in danger?

Source of information
- Problem observed by referrer
- Child talked to referrer
- Someone else told referrer of their concern – who?
- Referral has general concerns – why refer now?

Why is the referrer worried?
- Is there a need for immediate medical treatment?
- Is there a physical injury – size, colour, shape and location?
- Is the child neglected – appearance, clothing, home conditions?
- Is there a lack of supervision – whereabouts and situation of child?
- Is child a victim of sexual assault – child's account or behaviour?
- Is the child emotionally abused – observed behaviour?
- Is there a person present who has been convicted of an offence against a child?
- Is there an explanation?

Details of:
- Child's current whereabouts?
- Date child was last seen
- Any previous concerns
- Background to current concern
- Any specific injury or event causing concern

- When did it happen
- Child's, parent's/carer's account
- Identity of alleged abuser – personal details assist police checks
- Alleged abuser's current whereabouts
- Any supporting medical or forensic evidence

Is there any other possible explanation the referrer can offer for their concern?

Additional information
- Willingness of referrer to be interviewed
- Discrepancies or inconsistencies in the report

Family/household details

Child
Name, age, gender, ethnic origin, address and telephone number

Referrer
Name, address and telephone number

Referrer's Relationship to the child

Parent/carer
Name, address, telephone number and age if under 18 years

Access to parent/carer
Is an appointment necessary?

Alternative carer(s)
Name, address and telephone number

Other children in the household
Age and gender

Primary language of family

Ethnic origin of family

Religion of family

Disability of parent or child

Other professionals involved with the family

School/nursery
Address, telephone number and name of head teacher

Health visitor
Name, address and telephone number

General Practitioner
Name, address and telephone number

Probation Service
Name, address and telephone number

Any other

Is any other help needed?
Remember this is not a checklist. Record anything the referrer tells you about these or similar matters:
- Bereavement
- Child/parent conflict
- Drug/alcohol/ substance misuse
- Housing/homelessness
- Learning disability
- Non school attendance
- Physical disability
- Police involvement
- Racial harassment
- Violence
- Bullying
- Child behaviour
- Family/marital conflict
- Financial crisis
- Mental ill health
- Parenting
- Physical ill health
- Poverty
- Unemployment

Consider
- Is this the correct agency? – if not, refer elsewhere and tell referrer
- Have you sufficient information – if not where could you get more?
- Is the service available?
- Does the referrer want a visit immediately?
- Will an interpreter/sign language facilitator be needed?
- Are there mobility/access considerations?
- Are there any assurances you need to give? i.e. referrer's identity must be protected
- Feedback to the referrer about the action you will take
- How will you close the conversation – does anything else need saying, do they have any questions?
- Do you need to consult someone about the action to take?

Check
- Is the child/parent aware of the referral?
- Is the family/child known to the department?
- Is the family/child currently receiving services?
- If suspected child abuse – the Child Protection Register.

Useful telephone numbers
Record your most used telephone numbers here:

NSPCC © NSPCC 1998

First published 1998 by NSPCC, 42 Curtain Road, London, EC2A 3NH

NSPCC gives permission to photocopy this chart for use in connection with services to children and families. Published as part of a pack in the NSPCC Policy Practice Research Series: Assessing Risk in Child Protection, by Hedy Cleaver, Corinne Wattam, Pat Cawson (ISBN 0 902498 81 9).

Registered charity number 21640

Appendix

Using Assessments in Family Proceedings: Practice Issues

1.   There are a number of practice issues to which attention should be given in order to ensure that any information derived from assessment that is to be used in court proceedings conforms with court practice. These are set out below. Addressing these issues will assist legal practitioners, including the judiciary, and other professionals who may be involved in the case in giving proper weight to the conclusions reached during assessment.

2.   When preparing a report summarising evidence from the assessment, each page should be typed/word processed on one side of A4. The first page should be headed **Front Sheet** and include the following information:

- full name of child;
- date of birth;
- court case number;
- name of court hearing application;
- date of the court hearing;
- type of hearing (ie. directions, interim or final hearing);
- name of local authority;
- date of the report summarising the assessment.

Subsequent pages should also be singled sided. Headings and paragraph numbers will aid communication in court.

3.   It should be noted that the document submitted to court will usually be a summary of the key assessment issues rather than the full record concerning the assessment, as the latter will not usually be in a format or language suitable for court.

4.   Where during proceedings several assessments have been produced, the report to the court should identify each by a separate number to avoid confusion.

5.   Initial assessments, although incomplete, may sometimes be needed at an interim stage in the care proceedings. Reports to court on these initial assessments will not necessarily represent the local authority's comprehensive view that will be brought to the final hearing. It is therefore important that the front page of such an initial report, under **type of hearing**, should clearly distinguish between those for interim court

hearings and the report of the complete or core assessment prepared for the final hearing.

6. The last and separate page of the report of the assessment should include the following information:

- full name and professional position of the person who has prepared the report;

- this should normally be the social worker allocated to the case, although a range of other people within the authority and from other agencies may have contributed to aspects of the assessment;

- signature;

- date;

- work address and telephone number;

    Followed by

- local authority making the application;

- signature(s);

- date (s);

- work address(es) and telephone number(s).

7. The endorsement of the report of the assessment by the local authority raises similar issues to the approach commended in paragraphs 20–22 of LAC 99(29) *Care Plans and Care Proceedings Under the Children Act* 1989. The key point is that the report of the assessment is a statement by the local authority which is likely to be a crucial part of the authority's evidence in the care proceedings. However, it does not itself imply the commitment of resources across the local authority in the way care plans may do and, for this reason, endorsement at the level of a team manager may well be sufficient.

Appendix

E Data Protection Registrar's Checklist

Data Protection Registrar's Checklist for Setting up Information Sharing Arrangements (abridged version)

(i) What is the purpose of the information sharing arrangement?

1.　It is important in data protection terms that the purpose of any information sharing arrangement is clearly defined. This is because if *personal* information is to be disclosed, then disclosures must be registered with the Data Protection Registrar and the data protection principles will take effect. These principles themselves relate directly to the purpose or purposes for which personal information is held. For example, information must be adequate, relevant, and not excessive in relation to the purpose for which it is held, and must not be held longer than is necessary for that purpose.

2.　Parties to any arrangement should be aware that under the Data Protection Act 1998 they will need to have a 'legitimate basis' for disclosing sensitive personal data. The introduction of special controls on the processing of sensitive data (including holding and disclosing them) is one of the major innovations of the new Act. Under section 2, 'sensitive data' include information as to the commission, or alleged commission, by the data subject of any offence; and criminal proceedings involving the data subject as the accused, and their disposal. The definition of 'sensitive data' also includes information about the data subject's sexual life. It should also be made clear to all parties that information received under the arrangement is to be used only for the specified purpose(s). Thus, there should be a restriction on secondary use of personal data received under any information sharing arrangement *unless* the consent of the disclosing party to that secondary use is sought and granted.

(ii) Will it be necessary to share *personal* information in order to fulfil that purpose?

3.　Depersonalised information is information presented in such a way that individuals cannot be identified. If depersonalised information can be used to achieve the purpose, then there will be no data protection implications. Consideration should therefore always be given to whether the purpose can be achieved using depersonalised information; 'would failure to share personal information mean that the objectives of the arrangement could not be achieved?'

(iii) Do the parties to the arrangement have the *power* to disclose personal information for that purpose?

4. If the purpose cannot be achieved without sharing *personal* information, then each party to the arrangement will need to consider whether they have the power to disclose information for this purpose. This is particularly significant for public sector bodies or agencies whose powers and responsibilities are defined by statute or administrative law. If a public body acts *ultra vires* or outside its powers, then it may, at the same time, breach the lawfulness requirement of the first data protection principle. Section 115 of the Crime and Disorder Act 1998 may provide the parties with the lawful power they need provided the requirements of that section are met. This provides that any person can lawfully disclose information, where necessary or expedient for the purposes of any provision of the (1998) Act, to a chief officer of police, a police authority, local authorities, Probation Service or health authority, even if they do not otherwise have this power. This power also covers disclosure to people acting on behalf of any of the above named bodies. The 'purposes' of the Act referred to in Section 115 include a range of measures such as local crime audits, youth offending teams, anti-social behaviour orders, sex offender orders, and local child curfew schemes. It should also be noted that Section 17 of the Act places a statutory duty on every local authority to *exercise its various functions . . . with due regard to . . . the need to do all that it reasonably can to prevent . . . crime and disorder in its area.*

(iv) How *much* personal information will need to be shared in order to achieve the objectives of the arrangement?

5. Consideration must be given to the extent of any personal information disclosed. Some agencies may hold a lot of personal information on individuals but not all of this may be relevant to the purpose of the information sharing arrangement, so it may not be right to disclose it all. This is a matter for consideration by the agency holding the information.

(v) Should the *consent* of the individual be sought before disclosure is made?

6. When disclosing personal information, many of the data protection issues surrounding disclosure can be avoided if the consent of the individual has been sought and obtained. This is particularly significant if the personal information to be shared identified victims or witnesses where consideration should be given to any effects of disclosure of their personal data on third parties.

(vi) What if the consent of the individual is *not* sought, or is sought but *withheld*?

7. Consideration must be given to whether the personal information can be disclosed lawfully and fairly. In terms of *lawfulness*, an agency will need to consider whether personal information is held under a *duty of confidence*. If it is, then it may only be disclosed:

(a) with the individual's consent; or

(b) where there is an overriding public interest or justification for doing so.

It will not *always* be the case that the prevention and detection of crime or public safety constitutes an overriding public interest for the exchange of personal information.

8. As regards *fairness*, even if the personal information held is not subject to a duty of confidence, the agency will still need to consider how the disclosure can be made fairly. In data protection terms, in order to obtain and process personal data fairly, the individual should be informed of any non-obvious uses (including disclosure) of their personal data, and be given the opportunity to consent to those uses. If consent is therefore not obtained, consideration will have to be given to how the disclosure can be made fairly. This might involve arguments of public interest, but these would have to be balanced against any potential resulting prejudice to the interests of the individual concerned.

(vii) How does the non-disclosure *exemption* apply?

9. The Data Protection Acts 1984 and 1998 contain general 'non-disclosure provisions', but allow a number of specific exemptions. There is an exemption in both Acts which states that personal information may be disclosed for the purposes of the prevention or detection of crime, or the apprehension or prosecution of offenders, in cases where failure to disclose would be likely to prejudice those objectives. A party seeking to rely on this exemption needs to make a judgement as to whether, in the particular circumstances of an individual case, there would be a substantial chance that one or both of those objectives would be noticeably damaged if the personal information was withheld.

(viii) How do you ensure compliance with the *other data protection principles*?

10. Any information sharing arrangement should also address the following issues:

*   how will it be ensured that only the *minimum personal information necessary* is shared and held for the purpose(s) of the arrangement?

*   how will the *accuracy* of the personal information be maintained? One party to the arrangement may know that there has been a change in personal information which they have disclosed: how does that party ensure that all recipients of that personal information are kept informed of developments, so that they can keep their records up to date?

*   *for how long* will personal information be retained? It would be anomalous if the disclosing agency were to remove the personal information from its systems, but the other parties continued to hold it.

*   how will individuals be given *access* to personal information held about them? Under data protection legislation, individuals have a right of access to any information held about them. This right may be denied in certain limited circumstances, which include where access would prejudice the prevention or detection of crime. This could be significant, if, for example, a police force wished to disclose personal data to another party, but for operational reasons did not want the individual concerned to know the disclosure had been made. On the other hand, it is not sufficient to deny subject access merely because the information is held for

crime prevention purposes. Mechanisms must therefore be in place to ensure that the wishes of the disclosing party are considered.

- how will the personal data be *stored*? The more sensitive the personal data shared, the more security measures should be taken by each party receiving that personal data. This is not limited to physical security of the equipment on which it is held, but extends to technological security (for example, limited staff access, appropriate levels of staff access) and to staff security (staff with authorised access should be aware of its purpose and extent).

Appendix

F

Acknowledgements

Many people have helped in the development of the Assessment Framework and in shaping the Guidance in this volume and the associated materials. They have given generously of their time and expertise. Members of the Steering and Advisory Groups and critical readers have contributed their professional experience and management wisdom. A considerable debt is also owed to consultants from different disciplines who have worked closely with the Department of Health, especially Arnon Bentovim, Tony Cox and Steve Walker. Throughout there has been a strong collaborative effort involving Government Departments, the Open University, Royal Holloway College, the Universities of Sheffield and East Anglia, REU, Triangle, NSPCC, and many others. The development work has been marked by a collective commitment to improving outcomes for children and to assisting those critically important staff who daily work with children in need and their families.

In the chair of the Steering and Advisory Groups

Jenny Gray   Social Services Inspector, Department of Health

Consultant to the Project

Wendy Rose   Senior Research Fellow, The Open University

Members of the Steering Group

Sarah Bateman* Section Head (Child Protection), Department of Health (until August 1999)

Bruce Clark*   Director of Central Children's Services, National Council for the Prevention of Cruelty to Children (until August 1999) Section Head(Child Protection), Department of Health (from September 1999)

Jonathan Corbett* Social Services Inspector, National Assembly For Wales (from October 1999)

Chris Corrigan* Section Head (Family Support and Children in Need), Department of Health

Ann Gross*   Section Head (Quality Protects), Department of Health (until September 1999)

Steve Hart*	Social Services Inspector, Department of Health
Gillian Harrison	Head of Evidence and Procedures Section, Home Office
David Hill	Local Government Association and Head of Services (Children and Families), London Borough of Havering Social Services Department
Tom Jeffery	Branch Head, Children's Services, Department of Health
Dr Robert Jezzard*	Senior Policy Adviser, Department of Health
David Johnston*	Social Services Inspector, National Assembly For Wales (until September 1999)
Dr David Jones	Consultant Child and Family Psychiatrist, The Park Hospital, Oxford
Helen Jones*	Social Services Inspector, Department of Health
Dorothy Lewis	Regional Development Worker, Department of Health (from September 1999)
Margaret Lynch	Senior Policy Advisor, Department of Health (from September 1999)
Katrina McNamara*	Nursing Officer, Department of Health
Jeremy Oppenheim	Association of the Directors of Social Services and Director of Social Services, London Borough of Hackney (until August 1999)
Neil Remsbery	Team Leader (Special Educational Schools), Department for Education and Employment
Jennifer Ruddick*	Social Services Inspector, Department of Health
Kim Sibley *	Team Leader, Special Educational Needs Strategy Team, Department of Education and Employment
Gail Treml *	Professional Adviser, Special Educational Needs, Department of Education and Employment
Peter Smith*	Social Services Inspector, Department of Health
Andrew Webb	Association of the Directors of Social Services and Head of Children's Services, Cheshire County Council
Elizabeth Wulff-Cochrane	Development and Promotions Department, Central Council for the Education and Training of Social Workers

*also members of Advisory Group

Members of the Advisory Group

Jane Aldgate	Professor of Social Care, The Open University
Hedy Cleaver	Senior Research Fellow, Royal Holloway, University of London

Ratna Dutt OBE	Director, REU
Amanda Farr	Children's Services Manager, Milton Keynes County Council
Enid Hendry	Head of Child Protection Training, National Society for the Prevention of Cruelty to Children
Jan Horwath	Lecturer in Social Work, Department of Sociological Studies, University of Sheffield
Hugh McLaughlin	Assistant Director (Children and Families), Wigan Social Services Department
Jill Pedley	Assistant Director (Children and Families), Nottinghamshire Social Services Department
Melanie Phillips	Freelance Trainer, Researcher, Consultant to REU
Nigel Richardson	Assistant Director (Children and Families), Directorate of Social and Housing Services, North Lincolnshire Council
David Roberts	Team Leader, Health Services (Child Health), Department of Health
David Simpkins	Child Care Policy Officer, Devon Social Services Department
Ruth Sinclair	Director of Research, National Children's Bureau
June Thoburn	Professor of Social Work, University of East Anglia

Secretariat to the Project

Jim Brown	Policy Administrator, Department of Health
Dawn Tharpe	Secretary to Jenny Gray, Department of Health

Appendix

G

Bibliography

Adcock M (2000) *The Core Assessment: How to synthesise information and make judgements*. In Horwath J (ed) (2000) *The Child's World: Assessing Children in Need. The Reader*. The NSPCC, London.

Adcock M and White R (eds) (1998) *Significant Harm: its Management and Outcome*. Significant Publications, Croydon.

Aldgate J and Bradley M (1999) *Supporting Families Through Short Term Fostering*. The Stationery Office, London.

Belsky Y J and Vondra J (1989) *Lessons from child abuse: The determinants of parenting*. In Acchetti D and Carlson V (eds) (1989) *Child Maltreatment: Theory and Research on the Causes and Consequences of Child Abuse and Neglect*. Cambridge University Press, New York.

Bentovim A (1998) *Significant Harm in Context*. In Adcock M and White R (eds) (1998) *Significant Harm: its Management and Outcome*. pp. 57–89. Significant Publications, Croydon.

Bentovim A and Bingley Miller L (forthcoming) *Assessment of Family Competence, Strengths and Difficulties*.

Bentovim A, Elton A and Tranter M (1987) Prognosis for rehabilitation after abuse. *Adoption and Fostering*. **34**: 821–826.

Birleson P (1980) The validity of depressive disorder in childhood and the development of a self-rating scale: A research report. *Journal of Child Psychology and Psychiatry*. **22**: 73–88.

Bradley R and Caldwell B (1977) Home observation for measurement of the environment: A validation study of screening efficiency. *American Journal of Mental Deficiency*. **81**: 417-420.

Brandon M (1999) *Communicating with Children and Ascertaining their Wishes and Feelings*. In Shemmings D (1999) *In on the Act – A training programme for relevant professionals*. University of East Anglia, Norwich.

Brugha T, Bebington P, Tennant C and Hurry J (1985) The list of threatening experiences: A subset of 12 life event categories with considerable long-term contextual threat. *Psychological Medicine*. **15**: 189–194.

Butler I and Williamson H (1994) In NSPCC in association with Chailey Heritage and Department of Health (1997) *Turning Points: A Resource Pack for Communicating with Children. Introduction.* pp.1–2. The NSPCC, London.

Butt J and Box C (1998) *Family Centred. A study of the use of family centres by black families.* REU, London.

Caddle D and Crisp D (1997) *Imprisoned women and mothers.* Home Office Research Study 162. Home Office, London.

Caldwell B M and Bradley R H (1984) *Home Observation for Measurement of the Environment – Administration Manual (revised edition).* University of Arkansas, Arkansas.

Carers (Recognition and Services) Act 1995 (1995) HMSO, London.

Carers and Disabled Children Bill (2000) The Stationery Office, London.

Children Act 1989 (1989) HMSO, London.

Children Act 1989 (Amendment) Children's Services Planning Order 1996. Statutory Instrument 1996 No. 785. HMSO, London.

Children (Leaving Care) Bill (1999). The Stationery Office, London.

Cleaver H (2000) Fostering Family Contact: a study of children, parents and foster carers. The Stationery Office, London.

Cleaver H and Freeman P (1995) *Parental Perspectives in Cases of Suspected Child Abuse.* HMSO, London.

Cleaver H, Unell I and Aldgate J (1999) *Children's Needs – Parenting Capacity: The impact of parental mental illness, problem alcohol and drug use, and domestic violence on children's development.* The Stationery Office, London.

Cleaver H, Wattam C and Cawson P (1998) *Assessing Risk in Child Protection.* The NSPCC, London.

Compton B R and Galaway B (1989) *Social Work Processes.* Brookes Cole, Pacific Grove.

Connolly J and Shemmings D (1998) *Undertaking Assessments of Children and Families: A directory of training materials, courses and key texts.* University of East Anglia, Norwich.

Crime and Disorder Act 1998 (1998) The Stationery Office, London.

Crittenden P and Ainsworth MDS (1989) *Child Maltreatment and Attachment.* In Cicchetti D and Carlson V (eds) *Handbook of Child Maltreatment: Clinical and Theorectical Perspectives.* pp. 432–463. Cambridge, New York.

Crnic K A and Booth C L (1991) Mothers' and fathers' perceptions of daily hassles of parenting across early childhood. *Journal of Marriage and the Family.* 53: 1043–1050.

Crnic K A and Greenberg M T (1990) Minor parenting stresses with young children. *Child Development.* 61: 1628–1637.

Data Protection Act 1998 (1998) The Stationery Office, London.

Davie C E, Hutt S J, Vincent E and Mason M (1984) *The young child at home.* NFER-Nelson, Windsor.

Department for Education and Employment (1994) *Code of Practice on the Identification and Assessment of Special Educational Needs.* HMSO, London.

Department for Education and Employment (1999a) *School Inclusion: Pupil Support. The Secretary of State's guidance on pupil attendance, behaviour, exclusion and re-integration.* Circular No 10/99.

Department for Education and Employment (1999b) *Guidance on Assessment in the Learning Gateway for 16 and 17 year olds.* DfEE Publications (Ref: RDT/LG/9901).

Department for Education and Employment (2000) *Connexions: The best start in life for every young person.* DfEE Publications (Ref: CX2).

Department for Education and Employment and Department of Health (forthcoming) *Guidance on the Education of Children and Young People in Public Care.*

Department of Health (1988) *Protecting Children: A Guide for Social Workers Undertaking a Comprehensive Assessment.* HMSO, London.

Department of Health (1989) *An Introduction to the Children Act 1989.* HMSO, London.

Department of Health (1991) *The Children Act (1989) Guidance and Regulations. Volumes 1–10.* HMSO, London.

Department of Health, Social Services Inspectorate (1995a) *The Challenge of Partnership in Child Protection: Practice Guide.* HMSO, London.

Department of Health (1995b) *Looking After Children: Trial Pack of Planning and Review Forms and Assessment and Action Records (Revised).* HMSO, London.

Department of Health (1995c) *Looking After Children: Good Parenting, Good Outcomes. Training Guide.* HMSO, London.

Department of Health (1995d) *Child Protection: Messages from Research.* HMSO, London.

Department of Health, Social Services Inspectorate (1995e) *Growing up and moving on – transition services for disabled young people.* (CI(95)27). Department of Health, London.

Department of Health, Social Services Inspectorate (1995f) *Young Carers. Something to Think About.* (CI(96)38). Department of Health, London.

Department of Health (1996a) *Carers (Recognition and Services) Act 1995: Policy Guidance and Practice Guide.* Local Authority Circular LAC(97)7 and Health Services Guidelines HSG(96)8. Department of Health, London.

Department of Health, Social Services Inspectorate (1996b) *Standards Used by the Social Services Inspectorate, Volume 2: Children's Services, plus supplement to Vol 2. Children's Services* (CI(96)23). Department of Health, London.

Department of Health, Social Services Inspectorate (1996c) *Standards Used by the Social Services Inspectorate, Volume 3: Children's Residential Care, Secure Accommodation and Juvenile Justice.* (CI(96)23). Department of Health, London.

Department of Health, Social Services Inspectorate (1998a) *Young Carers: Making a Start.* Department of Health, London.

Department of Health (1998b) *National Priorities Guidance: A commitment to improve modern social services.* Department of Health, London.

Department of Health (1998c) *Adoption: Achieving the right balance.* Local Authority Circular LAC(98)20.

Department of Health (1998d) *Quality Protects Circular: Transforming Children's Services.* Local Authority Circular (LAC(98)28).

Department of Health (1998e) *Modernising social services: Promoting independence, Improving protection, Raising standards.* Department of Health, London.

Department of Health (1999a) *Caring about Carers: A National Strategy for Carers.* Department of Health, London.

Department of Health (1999b) *Children Looked After by Local Authorities. Year Ending 31 March 1998. England.* Government Statistical Services, London.

Department of Health (1999c) *Guidance to Local Authority Social Services Departments on Visits by Children to Special Hospitals.* Local Authority Circular (LAC(99)23).

Department of Health (1999d) *Care Plans and Care Proceedings under the Children Act 1989.* Local Authority Circular (LAC(99)29). Department of Health, London.

Department of Health (1999e) *The Government's Objectives for Children's Social Services.* Department of Health, London.

Department of Health (1999f) *Me, survive, out there?: new arrangements for young people living in and leaving care.* Department of Health, London.

Department of Health (1999g) *Adoption Now: Messages from Research.* Wiley, Chichester.

Department of Health (1999h) *Mental Health Act 1983 Code of Practice: Guidance on the visiting of psychiatric patients by children* (HSC1999/222 LAC(99)32). Department of Health, London.

Department of Health (1999i) *Children and Young People on Child Protection Registers. Year Ending 31 March 1999.* England. Government Statistical Service, London.

Department of Health (1999j) *Modernising Health and Social Services: National Priorities Guidance.* Department of Health, London.

Department of Health (1999k) *Social Services Performance in 1998–99. The Personal Social Services Performance Assessment Framework.* Local Authority Social Services LASSL(99)24. Department of Health, London.

Department of Health (2000a) *towards safer care. Training and Resource Pack.* Department of Health, London.

Department of Health (2000b) *Assessing Children in Need and their Families: Practice Guidance.* The Stationery Office, London.

Department of Health (2000c) *Studies which inform the development of the Framework for the Assessment of Children in Need and their Families.* The Stationery Office, London.

Department of Health (forthcoming, a) *Achieving Fair Access to Adult Social Care Services.*

Department of Health (forthcoming, b) *The Children Act 1989 Now: Messages from Research.* The Stationery Office, London.

Department of Health and Cleaver H (2000) *Assessment Recording Forms.* The Stationery Office, London.

Department of Health, Cox A and Bentovim A (2000) *The Family Assessment Pack of Questionnaires and Scales.* The Stationery Office, London.

Department of Health and Department for Education and Employment (1996) *Children's Services Planning Guidance.* Department of Health, London.

Department of Health and Department for Education and Employment (1999) *The Quality Protects Programme: Transforming Children's Services 2000/01.* Health Service Circular (HSC(99)237), Local Authority Circular (LAC(99)33) and DfEE Circular No. 18/99. Department of Health, London.

Department of Health, Dutt R and Phillips M (2000) *Improving identity and self-esteem for looked after children.* REU, London.

Department of Health, Home Office, Department for Education and Employment (1999) *Working Together to Safeguard Children: A guide to inter-agency working to safeguard and promote the welfare of children.* The Stationery Office, London.

Department of Health and The Local Government Association (1999) *Think Child! The councillor's guide to Quality Protects.* The Department of Health and the Local Government Assication, London.

Department of Health, University of Bristol, The NSPCC and Barnardos (1998) *Making an Impact: Children and Domestic Violence: Training Resource.* Barnardos, London.

Department of Health and The Welsh Office (1999) *Code of Practice Mental Health Act 1983.* The Stationery Office, London.

Dingwall R, Eekelaar J and Murray T (1983) *The protection of children: state intervention and family life.* Basil Blackwell, Oxford.

Disability Discrimination Act 1995 (1995) The Stationery Office, London.

Dutt R and Phillips M (2000) *The Assessment of Black Children in Need and their Families.* In Department of Health (2000b) *Assessing Children in Need and their Families: Practice Guidance.* The Stationery Office, London.

Education Act 1996 (1996) The Stationery Office, London.

Falkov A, Mayes K, Diggins M, Silverdale N and Cox A (1998) *Crossing Bridges – Training resources for working with mentally ill parents and their children.* Pavilion Publishing, Brighton.

The Family Proceedings Courts (Children Act 1989) Rules 1991 (SI 1395/1991 for Magistrates Courts and SI 1247/1991 for Higher Courts).

General Assembly of the United Nations (1989) *The Convention on the Rights of the Child.* Adopted by the General Assembly of the United Nations on 20 November 1989.

Goodman R (1997) The Strengths and Difficulties Questionnaire: A Research Note. *Journal of Child Psychology and Psychiatry.* **38**: 581-586.

Goodman R, Meltzer H and Bailey V (1998) The strengths and difficulties questionnaire: A pilot study on the validity of the self-report version. *European Child and Adolescent Psychiatry.* 7: 125–130.

Hardiker P, Exton K and Baker M (1996) The prevention of Child Abuse: a framework for analysing services. In *Childhood Matters: Report of the National Commission of Inquiry into the Prevention Of Child Abuse. Vol 2.* HMSO, London.

Hardiker P, Exton K and Barker M (1999) Children Still in Need, Indeed: prevention across five decades. In Stevenson O (1999) *Childhood Welfare in the UK.* Blackwell Science Ltd, Oxford

HM Prison Service (1994) *Release of Prisoners Convicted of Offences Against Children or Young Persons Under the Age of 18.* Instructions to Governors 54/1994.

HM Prison Service (1999) *Report of a review of principles, polices and procedures on mothers and babies/children in prison.* Women's Policy Unit, London.

HM Prison Service (2000) *Protocol: Additional Child Protection Arrangements for Under 18 years olds in Prison Service Establishments.* HM Prison Service, London.

Home Office (1998) *Speaking up for Justice Report of the Interdepartmental Working Group on the treatment of Vulnerable or Intimidated Witnesses in the Criminal Justice System.* The Stationery Office, London.

Home Office and Department of Health (1992) *Memorandum of Good Practice on Interviewing of Child Witnesses.* HMSO, London.

Home Office and Department of Health (1998) *Draft Guidance on Children Involved in Prostitution.* The Home Office, London.

Home Office and Department of Health (forthcoming) *Guidance on Children Involved in Prostitution.*

Horwath J (ed) (2000) *The Child's World: Assessing Children in Need. The Reader.* The NSPCC, London.

Human Rights Act 1998 (1998) The Stationery Office, London.

Howe D (2000) Attachment. In Horwath J (ed) (2000) *The Child's World: Assessing Children in Need. The Reader.* The NSPCC, London.

International Save the Children Alliance and United Nations High Commissioner for Refugees (1999) *Separated Children in Europe Programme, Statement of Good Practice.*

Jack G (1997) An Ecological Approach to Social Work with Children and Families. *Child and Family Social Work.* **2**: 109–120.

Jones D P H (1997) *Treatment of the child and the family where child abuse or neglect has occurred.* In Helfer R, Kempe R and Krugman R (eds) *The Battered Child, 5th edition.* pp.521–542. University of Chicago Press, Chicago.

Jones D P H (1998) *The effectiveness of intervention.* In Adcock M and White R (eds) (1998) *Significant Harm: its Management and Outcome.* pp. 91-119. Significant Publications, Croydon.

Jones D P H (2000) The Assessment of Parental Capacity. In Horwath J (ed) (2000) *The Child's World: Assessing Children in Need. The Reader.* The NSPCC, London.

Jones D P H (forthcoming) *Communicating with Children who may have been traumatised or maltreated.*

Jones D and Ramchandani P (1999) *Child Sexual Abuse: Informing Practice from Research.* Radcliffe Medical Press. Abingdon.

Kinston W and Loader P (1988) The Family Task Interview: A tool for clinical research in family interaction. *Journal of Marital and Family Therapy.* **14**: 67–87.

Local Government Bill (1999) The Stationery Office, London.

Marsh P and Peel M (1999) *Leaving Care in Partnership: family involvement with care leavers.* The Stationery Office, London.

Morris J (1999) *Move on Up: Supporting Young Disabled People in the Transition to Adulthood.* Barnardos, London.

Morris K, Marsh P and Wiffin J (1998) *Family Group Conferences – A Training Pack.* The Family Rights Group, London.

NHS (1999a) *The Visits by Children to Ashworth, Boradmoor and Rampton Hospitals Directions.* Health Service Circular (HSC1999/160).

NHS (1999b) *Mental Health Act 1983 Code of Practice: Guidance on the visiting of psychiatric patients by children.* Health Service Circular (HSC1999/222) and Local Authority Circular (LAC 99(32)).

The NSPCC in association with Chailey Heritage and Department of Health (1997) *Turning Points: A Resource Pack for Communicating with Children.* The NSPCC, London.

The NSPCC and the University of Sheffield (2000) *The Child's World: Assessing Children in Need. Training and Development Pack.* The NSPCC, London.

Office for National Statistics (1999) *Mental Health of Children and Adolescents.* Monograph series (99)409. Office for National Statistics, London.

Office for National Statistics (2000) *The development and well-being of children and adolescents in Great Britain.* Office for National Statistics, London.

Parker R M, Ward H, Jackson S, Aldgate J and Wedge P (eds) (1991) *Looking After Children: Assessing Outcomes in Children Care.* HMSO, London.

Pearn M, Roderick C and Mulrooney C (1995) *Learning Organisations in Practice.* McGraw-Hill, Maidenhead.

Piccinelli M, Tessari E, Bortolomasi M, Piasere O, Semenzin M, Garzotto N and Tansella M (1997) Efficacy of the alcohol use disorders identification test as a screening tool for hazardous alcohol intake and related disorders in primary care: A validity study. *British Medical Journal.* **514**: 420–424.

Ramsden S (1998) *Working with Children of Prisoners: A Resource for Teachers.* Save the Children, London.

Reder P and Duncan S (1999) *Lost Innocents.* Routledge, London.

Rutter M, Tizard J and Whitmore K (eds) (1970) *Education, Health and Behaviour.* Longmans, London.

Rutter M, Giller H and Hagell A (1998) *Anti-social Behaviour by Young People.* Cambridge University Press, Cambridge.

Ryan M (2000) *Working with Fathers.* Radcliffe Medical Press, Abingdon.

Schofield G (1998) Inner and outer worlds: a psychosocial framework for child and family social work. *Child and Family Social Work.* **3**, pp. 57–67.

Shemmings D (1999) *In on the Act – A Training Programme for Relevant Professionals.* School of Social Work, University of East Anglia, Norwich.

Silvester J, Bentovim A, Stratton P and Hanks H (1995) Using spoken attributions to classify abusive families. *Child Abuse and Neglect.* **19**(10):1221–1232.

Sinclair R, Garnett 1 and Berridge D (1995) *Social Work and Assessment with Adolescents.* National Children's Bureau, London.

Smith M A (1985) *The Effects of Low Levels of Lead on Urban Children: The relevance of social factors.* Ph.D. Psychology, University of London.

Snaith R P, Constantopoulos A A, Jardine M Y and McGuffin P (1978) A clinical scale for the self-assessment of irritability. *British Journal of Psychiatry.* **132**: 164–171.

Social Exclusion Unit (1998) *Bringing Britain Together: A National Strategy for Neighbourhood Renewal.* The Stationery Office, London.

Social Exclusion Unit (1999) *Bridging the Gap: New opportunities for 16–18 year olds not in education, employment or training.* The Stationery Office, London.

Social Services Inspectorate and Surrey County Council (1995) *Unaccompanied Asylum-Seeking Children: A Training Pack.* Department of Health, London.

Stevenson O (1998) *Neglected Children: Issues and Dilemmas.* Blackwell Science, Oxford.

Thomas T and Beckford V (1999) *Adopted Children Speaking*. BAAF, London.

Tunstill J and Aldgate J (2000) *From Policy to Practice: Services for Children in Need*. The Stationery Office, London.

Utting D (1995) *Family and Parenthood: Supporting Families, Preventing Breakdown*. Joseph Rowntree Foundation, York.

Varma V (ed) (1993) *How and Why Children Fail*. Cassell, London.

Ward H (ed) (1995) *Looking After Children: Research into Practice: The Second Report of the Department of Health on Assessing Outcomes in Child Care*. HMSO, London.

Youth Justice and Criminal Evidence Act 1999 (1999). The Stationery Office, London